Collins

Key Stage 3

Early Modern

British and World History

1509–1760

2nd edition

Laura Aitken-Burt, Robert Peal and Robert Selth

Published by Collins
An imprint of HarperCollins*Publishers*
The News Building, 1 London Bridge Street, London, SE1 9GF, UK

HarperCollins*Publishers*
Macken House, 39/40 Mayor Street Upper,
Dublin 1, D01 C9W8, Ireland

Browse the complete Collins catalogue at
collins.co.uk

ISBN 978-0-00-849205-2

British Library Cataloguing-in-Publication Data

A catalogue record for this publication is available from the British Library.

Authors: Laura Aitken-Burt, Robert Peal and Robert Selth
Series editor: Robert Peal
Publisher: Katie Sergeant
Product manager: Joanna Ramsay
Editor: Caroline Low
Fact-checker: Barbara Hibbert
Proof-reader: David Hemsley
Cover designer: Gordon MacGilp
Cover image: Deco / Alamy Stock Photo
Typesetter: QBS
Production controller: Alhady Ali
Printed in India by Multivista Global Pvt. Ltd.

Acknowledgements
The publishers gratefully acknowledge the permission granted to reproduce the copyright material in this book. Every effort has been made to trace copyright holders and to obtain their permission for the use of copyright material. The publishers will gladly receive any information enabling them to rectify any error or omission at the first opportunity.

Contents

Introduction

'Printing, gunpowder and the compass: These three have changed the whole face and state of things throughout the world; the first in literature, the second in warfare, the third in navigation; whence have followed innumerable changes...'

Francis Bacon, *Novum Organum*, 1620

Book 2 of Knowing History covers the Early Modern period, an age when expanding empires and new technologies accelerated global change. Civilisations that first mastered the use of gunpowder were able to increase their power across the globe with terrifying speed. New ideas and religions spread at an unprecedented pace, thanks to the invention of the printing press. This book will help you understand the impact of these changes, from the Royal Court of Henry VIII to the battlefields of the English Civil War, via Renaissance Italy and Edo Japan.

The book is split evenly between British and World History. The British History units begin with the coronation of Henry VIII in 1509, when England was a small Catholic country ruled by the Tudors. The story ends in 1760, when England was part of a newly created Protestant country called Great Britain, ruled by the Georgians and on the cusp of becoming a global empire. Along the way, you will learn how Parliament, having nearly been blown up by Guy Fawkes, overtook the monarchy to become the most powerful institution in the land.

In terms of global history, you will learn how the world was transformed by contact between Europe and the Americas. Cultures, foods and diseases that had always been separated by the Atlantic Ocean collided in a process that was both extraordinary and devastating. In Asia, you will learn how the great Empires of the Ottomans and the Mughals thrived on expansion and trade, while Edo Japan spent two centuries largely cut off from the rest of the world. In Renaissance Europe, intellectual explorers celebrated the past, reviving the cultures of Ancient Greece and Rome for a new age.

In studying these dramatic religious, political and geographical changes, you will have a front row seat in the unveiling of the modern world. Where this book starts, Catholicism was the only religion in Western Europe, the Mughal Empire was yet to be founded, and nobody outside of the Americas had ever tasted chocolate. Breakthroughs in global travel and technology meant that by the end of this period in 1760, a very different world had appeared.

The world we live in today emerged because of what happened in the past. In studying history, you may even start to see events in the present mirroring events in the past. As it is often said, history does not repeat itself, but it does sometimes rhyme.

Robert Peal, series editor and co-author of Knowing History

Concise chapter introductions set the scene for each topic.

Photographs, maps and artwork illustrate and embed key concepts.

Fact boxes provide interesting, bite-sized information and details.

Check your understanding questions at the end of every chapter allow you to check and consolidate your learning.

Timelines map out the key dates from the unit, and help you understand the course of events. There is also a full timeline of events from across the units at the end of the book.

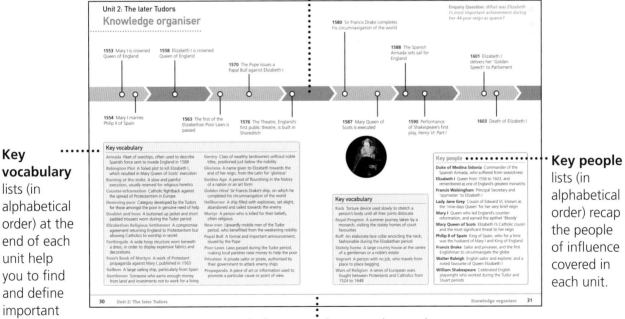

Key vocabulary lists (in alphabetical order) at the end of each unit help you to find and define important terminology.

Key people lists (in alphabetical order) recap the people of influence covered in each unit.

Knowledge organisers can be used to revise and quiz yourself on key dates, people and definitions.

Unit 1: Henry VIII and the Reformation
The young Henry VIII

When Henry VIII was crowned king in 1509, he was already the hero of **Tudor** England. He was tall and handsome, and a keen jouster, wrestler, archer, hunter and tennis player.

Henry VIII was taught by some of the greatest philosophers of the age, and could write poetry, compose music and speak French and Latin fluently. The scholar Thomas More wrote a poem to celebrate Henry's coronation, stating: "This day is the end of our slavery, the fount of liberty; the end of sadness, the beginning of joy". High hopes rested on the young king's shoulders.

Henry was not meant to be king, but he became heir to the throne aged 10 when his older brother Arthur died unexpectedly in 1502. When his father Henry VII died, Henry VIII inherited the throne. Straight away, Henry married his dead brother's widow, Catherine of Aragon. Catherine was a Spanish princess six years his senior. Her powerful parents had recently united Spain as a single kingdom, and Henry's marriage secured England's alliance with this newly powerful nation.

Henry was 17 years old when he became king. He ruled over a magnificent court, with continual entertainments and parties. Henry ordered regular jousting tournaments, which he often took part in himself. However, all this jousting had a serious purpose: Henry VIII was training his noblemen for war. The new king dreamed of conquest, transforming England into a great European empire, ruling over Wales, Scotland, Ireland and France.

Portrait of Henry VIII, painted shortly after his coronation

War with France

Having allied with Spain and the **Holy Roman Empire**, Henry invaded France in 1513. The English army captured two towns, and won a victory against the French at the Battle of the Spurs. Henry's allies had changed their minds, however, and decided not to invade France. This left the English army unable to advance any further. Henry signed a peace treaty with France, securing new lands and an annual payment for England.

During the invasion of France, the Scottish King James IV (who was allied with France) took the opportunity to invade northern England with a large army of 60 000 men. With Henry absent, Queen Catherine organised England's defence against the Scots. The Scottish army was soundly beaten at the Battle of Flodden with thousands killed, including the Scottish King James IV. Catherine organised for the Scottish king's bloodstained tunic to be sent as a gift to Henry VIII in France.

The Field of the Cloth of Gold

Victories over the French and Scottish in 1513 confirmed England's position as a major European power. Henry VIII's dream of empire was edging ever closer. But events took a bad turn in 1516 when France gained a new king, the warlike and shrewd Francis I. Henry's **Lord Chancellor**, Thomas Wolsey (see box), persuaded Henry to make peace with France.

> Fact
>
> Henry had an older sister named Margaret, but she could not inherit the English throne due to the law of male **primogeniture**. This law gave preference to sons inheriting the crown rather than daughters, and lasted until the Succession of the Crown Act in 2013.

Henry was reluctant to let go of his ambitions. To make the peace between England and France seem more honourable, Wolsey organised a magnificent celebration of peace. In June 1520, Henry VIII and Francis I met in France. For two weeks the young kings tried to outdo each other with displays of wealth and flamboyance. Henry and Francis even met each other in the wrestling ring, where Francis I won, much to Henry's anger. Many of the tents in which the visitors stayed were made from cloth threaded with gold, so the event became known as the 'Field of the Cloth of Gold'.

The Field of the Cloth of Gold, painted for Henry VIII in 1545

Thomas Wolsey

Masterminding Henry VIII's early successes was a priest named Thomas Wolsey. The son of an Ipswich butcher, Wolsey rose from humble beginnings to become the most powerful man in England, aside from the king.

In 1514 Wolsey became Archbishop of York. The following year, the Pope made him a **Cardinal** and Henry appointed him Lord Chancellor, the king's chief advisor. Through sheer drive, Wolsey had gained complete control of English politics and the church. He worked tirelessly, organising the affairs of state so that Henry could enjoy himself. Whatever the king wanted, Wolsey would deliver.

Wolsey became magnificently rich, and liked to show off his wealth, travelling through London each morning in a grand procession flanked by two silver crosses. He built himself a house beside the River Thames, which was grander and larger than any belonging to the king. Wolsey named it **Hampton Court** Palace. Many in Henry's court were envious of Wolsey, resenting the fact that this 'butcher's boy' had risen to such wealth and power. His enemies nicknamed him the 'fat maggot', and began to plot his downfall.

Check your understanding

1. Who was Henry VIII's first wife, Catherine of Aragon, previously married to?
2. What military successes did England enjoy in 1513?
3. Why did Cardinal Wolsey persuade Henry VIII to make peace with France?
4. What was the purpose of the Field of the Cloth of Gold celebrations in 1520?
5. What positions of power did Thomas Wolsey hold?

The Reformation

At the start of the 16th century, the Roman Catholic Church was the single most powerful organisation in Western Europe.

From the forests of Poland in the east, to the coast of Portugal in the west, this one religion held sway over millions of lives. At the head of the Catholic Church was the Pope, who lived in Rome and controlled a large swathe of central Italy. Catholics believed that the Pope was God's representative on Earth, and he held enormous power. During the medieval period, popes called for crusades, started wars, and could make or break European royal families. However, by 1500, the Roman Catholic Church had developed a reputation for **corruption**.

Corruption

The papacy had been taken over by wealthy, power-hungry popes who paid little attention to religion. Perhaps the most infamous was Pope Alexander VI, who was from a powerful Spanish family known as the Borgias. He threw all-night parties, stole money from the church, and had as many as ten children with his mistresses – even though the Pope, as a Catholic clergyman, was supposed to remain **celibate**.

In order to raise money, the Catholic Church sold **indulgences**. An indulgence was a certificate personally signed by the Pope, which a Christian could buy to gain forgiveness for their sins. You could even buy indulgences for dead relatives, to shorten their time in purgatory.

There was also a lively market for 'holy **relics**'. Normally said to be body parts of saints or Jesus Christ, these relics were rarely genuine. Churches would buy and sell the fingernail of Jesus Christ, part of the tree from the Garden of Eden, or a vial of the Virgin Mary's breast milk. Pilgrims would pay churches considerable amounts of money to see and touch these relics, believing they had divine powers.

Pope Alexander VI

Lastly, the Catholic Church was enormously wealthy. Even holy orders of nuns and monks, who were supposed to live a life of simplicity and poverty in monasteries and abbeys, could be found living in luxury. The Catholic clergy wore **vestments** made of finest silk and velvet, and Catholic churches were richly decorated, with gold **altars**, wall paintings, burning **incense** and **stained glass** windows.

Protestantism

Some priests began to argue that the Catholic Church had strayed from the true word of Jesus Christ, and been turned rotten by wealth. Jesus Christ lived a life of simplicity and

Money was raised to build St Peter's Basilica in the Vatican from the sale of indulgences

preached against greed, they argued, so should the Catholic Church not follow his example?

These priests attacked the Pope and the Catholic Church, giving sermons and writing short books explaining their beliefs. They were greatly aided by the newly invented printing press (see Unit 6, Chapter 3), which allowed their books to spread throughout Europe. Due to their 'protest' against the authority of the Catholic Church, they were given the name 'Protestants'.

Protestantism was particularly powerful in Germany, Switzerland, Holland and Belgium, where priests such as John Calvin and Martin Luther (see box) gained large followings. They proposed a simpler form of Christianity, replacing ritual and superstition with the word of the Bible, and richly decorated church interiors with plain, whitewashed walls.

Fundamental to Protestantism was the belief that all Christians should have their own relationship with God, formed through regular reading of the Bible. However, within Roman **Catholicism** the Bible could only be read in Greek, Hebrew or Latin, and all services were conducted in Latin. So, in secret, Protestants began translating the Bible into their own languages. This movement to reform Christianity spread across Europe and became known as 'the **Reformation**'.

Fact

Counting up all of the relics from a particular saint, one Protestant tract concluded that the saint must have had six arms, and 26 fingers.

Martin Luther

Born in Germany, Martin Luther became a monk at the age of 22. In 1510 he visited Rome, and was appalled by the wealth and corruption that he saw there.

In 1517 Luther wrote a list of arguments, known as the '95 theses', attacking church abuses, in particular the selling of indulgences. Luther nailed the 95 theses to the door of his church in Wittenberg, and this event is often said to have marked the start of the Reformation. In 1522, at a meeting known as the Diet of Worms, Pope Leo X declared Luther a **heretic** and an outlaw. On leaving the court, Luther was ambushed and kidnapped. However, his kidnapper was a German prince who offered Luther a hiding place at Wartburg Castle. In 1525, Luther married a former nun named Katharina von Bora who had abandoned her convent. Together they had six children. Luther also began to translate the Bible into German. He finished his German Bible in 1534, by which time much of Germany had converted to Protestantism.

Modern illustration of Martin Luther and his 95 theses

Check your understanding

1. Why was Pope Alexander VI so infamous?
2. What was corrupt about the selling of indulgences?
3. How were Protestant churches different from Catholic churches?
4. Why did Protestants want to translate the Bible into their own languages?
5. What did Martin Luther do in 1517, which is said to have marked the start of the Reformation?

Henry's 'Great Matter'

In 1522 Henry VIII invaded France again, only to be embarrassed when his ally, the Holy Roman Emperor Charles V, failed to turn up.

Catherine of Aragon

When Henry tried to raise money for another invasion in 1525, there were riots across England, so the invasion had to be called off. Henry's hopes of conquering France were abandoned, and he was left humiliated and frustrated.

Henry's frustration off the battlefield was even more serious. His wife, Catherine of Aragon, was now 40 years old and had given him only one child who survived infancy – his daughter Mary. Henry desperately wanted a male heir to continue the Tudor royal line, but by 1525 Catherine was unlikely to provide one.

By now, Henry had fallen in love with a younger, prettier woman called Anne Boleyn, who was a **lady-in-waiting** to Queen Catherine. Anne was highly educated, ambitious and flirtatious, teasing Henry that she would only make love to him if he took her as his wife. As part of the **royal court**, she was able to enrapture the king with her intelligence and wit. Before long, Henry was desperate to have Anne as his wife.

Anne Boleyn

The 'Great Matter'

In order to marry Anne, Henry first had to divorce Catherine. But this had to be approved by Pope Clement. Unfortunately for Henry, Catherine of Aragon's nephew was the Holy Roman Emperor Charles V. He had recently captured Rome, taking Pope Clement as his prisoner. Charles ordered that on no account should Pope Clement allow Henry to divorce his aunt Catherine, and Clement obeyed.

Henry was absolutely determined to gain a divorce, and called the issue his 'Great Matter'. He claimed that he had solid, religious grounds to do so. The book of Leviticus in the Bible states if a man marries his brother's widow, the couple will remain childless. Henry used this passage to argue

Modern illustration of Catherine of Aragon pleading her case against divorce

that his marriage to Catherine was never lawful in the first place, and God had cursed him by not providing a son. Catherine defended her position as Queen with equally forceful arguments against Henry's claims. In 1527, Henry asked Pope Clement to annul his marriage, but the Pope refused.

Henry asked his Chancellor Thomas Wolsey to persuade the Pope to change his mind. However, even the supremely powerful Cardinal Wolsey failed to do so.

Henry was furious, and Wolsey rapidly fell from favour. To try to win back the king, Wolsey gave him his magnificent Hampton Court Palace as a gift, but it was not enough. Wolsey was stripped of his job as Lord Chancellor in 1529, and fled to York. In 1530 he was ordered to stand trial on a trumped-up charge of treason. During his journey from York back to London, Wolsey died a broken man. With his last words, Wolsey said: "If I had served God as diligently as I have done the King, he would not have given me over in my grey hairs. How be it this is just reward…?"

The break with Rome

For six long years, Henry tried and failed to get his divorce, but then he had a new idea. Anne Boleyn was a keen reader of Martin Luther's books. She, and many others, suggested to the king that if England were no longer a Catholic country, Henry would no longer need the Pope's approval to divorce.

The Great Gatehouse at Hampton Court Palace

Henry did not like Protestant ideas. In 1521, he wrote a book entitled *Defence of the Seven Sacraments*, which attacked Luther's ideas and defended the Pope. Henry had made it illegal to own Luther's books. He even burnt suspected Protestants at the stake for being heretics. Henry VIII's early defence of Catholicism earned him the title 'Defender of the Faith' from Pope Leo X.

However, as Henry was desperate for a divorce, and furious with the Pope, he began to see some benefits in Protestant ideas. He also realised that if the head of the English Church was not the Pope, it could be him.

In January 1533, Henry married Anne Boleyn in secret. The marriage was declared valid by the Archbishop of Canterbury, Thomas Cranmer, two months later. Then, in November 1534, Parliament passed the **Act of Supremacy**, one of the most important laws in English history. It confirmed England's **break with Rome**, and created a new Church of England. From now on, England no longer belonged to the Roman Catholic Church, and Henry VIII was the **Supreme Head of the Church of England**.

> ### Fact
>
> Anne Boleyn had such a strong hold over the king's affection that many myths grew up around her. Some said she had six fingers and that she was a witch.

Check your understanding

1. Why was Henry VIII so dissatisfied with his marriage to Catherine of Aragon by 1525?
2. What prevented Henry VIII from being able to divorce Catherine of Aragon, and marry Anne Boleyn?
3. On what grounds did Henry VIII claim that his first marriage was not lawful?
4. Why did leaving the Roman Catholic Church provide a solution to Henry VIII's 'Great Matter'?
5. What did the 1534 Act of Supremacy confirm?

The English Reformation

To ensure full support for the Act of Supremacy, Henry VIII ordered that all public figures and clergymen swear the **Oath of Supremacy.**

This oath stated that Henry was the Supreme Head of the Church of England. Those who refused to swear were tried for treason and executed.

A group of Carthusian monks who were loyal to the Pope were among those who refused. As punishment, they were dragged through the streets of London, then hanged, drawn and quartered at Tyburn. The abbot's arm was brought back to the abbey, and nailed to the door. The monks' heads were placed on the spikes above London Bridge.

The most famous figure to refuse was Henry's great friend Sir Thomas More, who was one of the most celebrated writers and thinkers in England. More became Lord Chancellor after the downfall of Thomas Wolsey, but only lasted three years before stepping down in 1532. As a devout Roman Catholic, More could not accept Henry's marriage to Anne. In 1534 he refused to swear the Oath of Supremacy, and was locked in a dark, damp prison cell for 17 months. Henry pleaded with More to swear the Oath, but his conscience would not allow him to change his mind. More was tried for treason and executed in 1535. On the scaffold, More said: "I die the king's good servant, but God's servant first".

Thomas More, Lord Chancellor to Henry VIII until 1532

The Dissolution of the Monasteries

With Thomas Wolsey dead, and Sir Thomas More executed, Henry needed a new chief minister. He chose Thomas Cromwell, who was born the son of a Putney blacksmith, but rose to become Chancellor of the Exchequer. Cromwell had led an exciting life, working as a **mercenary**, wool merchant, banker and lawyer along the way.

A keen reader of Luther, Cromwell pushed for further Protestant reforms to the church. In particular, he proposed that all of England's monasteries and abbeys should be closed down. Monasteries had a 1000-year history of providing education, prayer and charity to the people of England. But they were also accused of excessive wealth and corruption. Many of England's 800 monasteries were enormously wealthy, owning magnificent treasures and a quarter of the land in England. If they were closed, Cromwell told Henry, this land and property would revert to the crown. Henry was in urgent need of money to fight more wars, so the **dissolution of the monasteries** began in 1536.

Ruins of Whitby Abbey, in Yorkshire England

The king's men descended on the monasteries, stripping lead from their roofs, gold, silver and jewels from their altars, and selling their land to local landowners. Monks and nuns were given a small pension, and turned out onto the streets. Henry made himself enormously rich, increasing the crown's income by around £150 000 a year (perhaps £80 million in today's money). England's monasteries, once so magnificent, were left to crumble – the haunting ruins of these ancient buildings can still be seen across England today.

The Pilgrimage of Grace

For many in England, the destruction of England's monasteries was a step too far. In autumn 1536, a group of angry Catholics gathered together in Yorkshire, led by a young nobleman named Robert Aske. He and his followers occupied York. They then invited the expelled nuns and monks to return to their monasteries and resume Catholic observance.

Banner carried during the Pilgrimage of Grace, showing the Holy Wounds of Jesus Christ

Aske's followers became known as the 'Pilgrimage of Grace', and their numbers swelled to around 35 000 men. Many were armed, and they planned to march on London.

Henry VIII sent an army north to meet Aske and his rebel army. He promised that if they went home, they would be forgiven. However, Henry was growing increasingly cruel. A year later, when a much smaller rebellion took place, he took the opportunity to round up and kill 200 of those involved in Aske's rebellion. In Cumberland, 70 villagers were hanged from trees in their villages in front of their families. Robert Aske was hanged in chains from York Castle, and left to die in agonising pain.

Tudor schools

Before their dissolution, monasteries provided a basic education for boys from the surrounding area. To replace this service, wealthy businessmen and landowners established new 'grammar schools'. Over 300 such schools were established during the 16th century, with a strong focus on teaching Latin grammar and promoting the new Protestant faith. Many were named after Henry VIII's son, King Edward VI, and his daughter Queen Elizabeth I. However, girls were not allowed to attend these schools. Some noble families did educate their daughters, but most were expected to remain at home and learn from their mothers how to manage a household and raise children.

The school day normally stretched from 7 a.m. to 5 p.m. The main subjects were Latin, religion, arithmetic and music. Boys would write with a quill pen, made from a trimmed feather. Misbehaving pupils would be beaten with a birch, or rapped over the knuckles with a wooden rod.

Check your understanding

1. What happened to those in England who refused to swear the Oath of Supremacy?
2. Who was Thomas Cromwell, and what were his religious views?
3. How did Henry VIII gain from the Dissolution of the Monasteries?
4. Why did Robert Aske begin the Pilgrimage of Grace?
5. Why did the Dissolution of the Monasteries lead to the creation of so many new schools in England?

Henry VIII and Edward VI

Henry VIII's marriage to Anne Boleyn did not last long. Her independent character, which had so delighted Henry when he first met her, infuriated him once she was his wife.

Henry longed for a son, but when Anne gave birth in September 1533, the child was a girl. She was named Elizabeth after Henry's mother. However, Henry was so disappointed not to have a male heir, he refused to attend his daughter Elizabeth's christening.

Anne miscarried her next three children, and Henry's dislike for her grew. After three years of marriage, Anne was charged with multiple cases of adultery and treason, though she was almost certainly innocent. In May 1536, Anne was executed, along with four of her accused lovers. One day later, Henry became engaged to his third wife, Jane Seymour. Henry adored Jane and in 1537 she provided Henry with the son he had always desired. They named him Edward.

Jane died soon after Edward's birth, and Henry went on to have three more wives but no more children. In 1540, he married Anne of Cleves, but there was little attraction between them and they divorced six months later. Later that year the now 49-year-old Henry married seventeen-year-old lady-in-waiting Catherine Howard, but she was accused of adultery and beheaded in 1541. Finally, in 1543 Henry married Catherine Parr, who acted as a stepmother to his three children, and outlived Henry.

Jane Seymour   Anne of Cleves

Catherine Howard Catherine Parr

Henry the tyrant

During a jousting tournament at Greenwich Palace in 1536, Henry was crushed beneath his horse and suffered severe injuries. Unable to exercise, he grew enormously fat and developed a 54-inch waist, arthritis and painful ulcers. By the end of his life Henry was too overweight to walk, and had to be wheeled around his palace in a specially made machine.

During this period, Henry turned against Protestant ideas, and put the English Reformation into reverse. In 1539, Parliament passed the Six Articles, reasserting Catholic doctrines such as celibate priests and **transubstantiation**. A year later, Henry beheaded his chief minister Thomas Cromwell for his Protestant sympathies, and for organising Henry's failed marriage to Anne of Cleves.

Henry was becoming increasingly tyrannical, and between 1532 and 1540 he executed 330 people: Protestants were burnt at the stake for being heretics; Catholics were hanged, drawn and quartered for being traitors; and the king's relatives were beheaded for being seen as rivals to the throne. In 1531, Henry VIII passed a law ruling that murderers who used poison should be boiled to death.

> ### Fact
>
> Catherine Parr published a book of Protestant prayers in 1545, making her the first ever woman to write a book in English under her own name. The following year, Henry nearly arrested her for heresy before changing his mind.

On 28 January 1547, Henry died aged 55. His funeral was a full Catholic service, complete with incense and Latin chanting. By the end of his long and eventful reign, Henry had invaded France three times, married six different wives, executed a Lord Chancellor and a chief minister, amassed 55 royal palaces, founded the Royal Navy, made himself King of Ireland, and established the Church of England.

Edward VI

Following his death, Henry's only surviving son Edward became king. Edward was just nine years old. Known as the 'boy king' and the 'godly imp', Edward VI was very intelligent, and a far stronger believer in the Reformation than his father. Whilst Henry VIII had started the English Reformation, the Church of England remained Catholic throughout his reign. It simply did not recognise the authority of the Pope in Rome.

Edward VI passed further Protestant reforms to the English Church: priests were allowed to marry; the Catholic **Mass** was abolished; and church services in English became compulsory. He also authorised the first prayer book in English, Thomas Cranmer's **Book of Common Prayer**.

Portrait of Edward VI

However, Edward was an unhealthy and weak child. Aged only 15, sores appeared across his body and he began to cough up blood. In 1553 Edward died, unmarried and childless. Henry VIII's nightmare of an unstable throne with no certain heir had become a reality.

The end of the old faith

Once on the throne, Edward VI was advised by his uncle, the Duke of Somerset, and his strongly Protestant Archbishop of Canterbury, Thomas Cranmer.

Any remaining Catholic features were rooted out of English churches. Altars, hanging crucifixes, shrines, rood screens and statues were burned, while stained glass windows were smashed and wall paintings whitewashed. Catholic rituals and ceremonies, such as Corpus Christi processions and 'creeping to the cross', were banned. To most of England's poor, illiterate population, these colourful practices were fundamental to their belief, but from now on, they were deprived of the religion they knew and loved.

Rosaries, holy water, relics and icons were all banned from the Church of England. The old faith of medieval England had gone, and in its place was a new religion based not on ritual and superstition, but on the word of the Bible.

Modern image of a wooden rosary

Check your understanding

1. On what grounds was Anne Boleyn executed in 1536?
2. Was Henry VIII's marriage to Jane Seymour a success?
3. How did Henry VIII's accident in 1536 change his appearance?
4. Why did Henry VIII execute his chief minister Thomas Cromwell in 1540?
5. How were Edward VI's religious views different from those of his father?

Unit 1: Henry VIII and the Reformation
Knowledge organiser

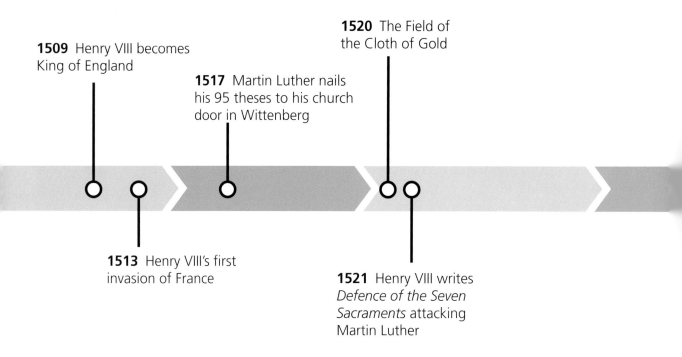

1509 Henry VIII becomes King of England

1520 The Field of the Cloth of Gold

1517 Martin Luther nails his 95 theses to his church door in Wittenberg

1513 Henry VIII's first invasion of France

1521 Henry VIII writes *Defence of the Seven Sacraments* attacking Martin Luther

---

Key vocabulary

Act of Supremacy A law passed by Parliament which led to the creation of the Church of England

Altar The table in a Christian church where the priest performs the Holy Communion

Book of Common Prayer A book of prayers used for Church of England services and written in English

Break with Rome England's decision to leave the Roman Catholic Church in 1534

Cardinal A senior member of the Catholic Church, who wears a distinctive red cassock

Catholicism One of the three major branches of Christianity, led from Rome by the Pope

Celibate Choosing to remain unmarried and abstain from sex, usually for religious reasons

Corruption The misuse of power for dishonest or immoral purposes

Dissolution of the Monasteries The closure of all religious houses in England by Henry VIII

Hampton Court A magnificent palace built by Thomas Wolsey, and later given as a gift to King Henry VIII

Heretic Someone with beliefs that question or contradict the established church

Holy Roman Empire A collection of central European states that developed during the medieval period

Incense A substance made from tree resin, burnt in churches to create a strong sweet aroma

Indulgence A forgiveness of one's sins purchased from the medieval Catholic Church

Lady-in-waiting A female member of the Royal Court, working as a personal assistant to the Queen

Lord Chancellor The king's most powerful advisor, also known as 'keeper of the Great Seal'

Mass The central act of worship in the Catholic Church, when the Holy Communion is taken

Mercenary A professional soldier who is paid to fight for foreign armies

Oath of Supremacy An oath of allegiance to the monarch as supreme head of the Church of England

Primogeniture Rule by which royal or noble lands and titles are inherited by the eldest child

Protestantism A form of Christianity which emerged during the 1500s in protest against Catholicism

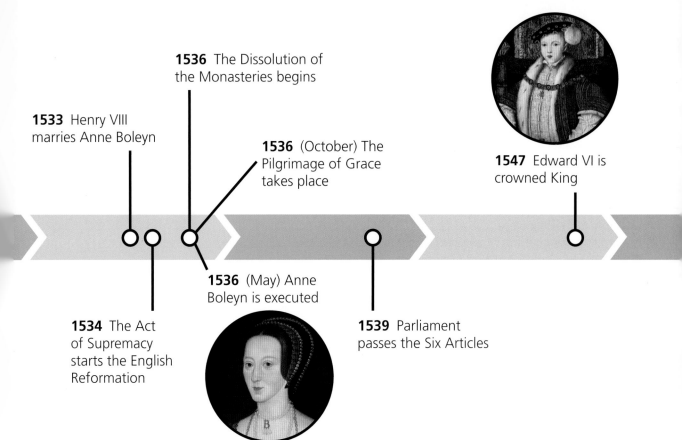

1536 The Dissolution of the Monasteries begins

1533 Henry VIII marries Anne Boleyn

1536 (October) The Pilgrimage of Grace takes place

1547 Edward VI is crowned King

1536 (May) Anne Boleyn is executed

1534 The Act of Supremacy starts the English Reformation

1539 Parliament passes the Six Articles

Key vocabulary

Reformation A movement to reform the Christian church which began with Martin Luther in Germany

Relic An object of religious significance, often the physical or personal remains of a saint

Royal Court A collection of nobles and clergymen, known as courtiers, who advise the monarch

Stained glass Decorative coloured glass, often found in the windows of churches and cathedrals

Supreme Head of the Church of England The title granted to Henry VIII following the Act of Supremacy

Transubstantiation The change of bread and wine into the body and blood of Christ during Communion

Tudors The royal dynasty that ruled England from 1485 to 1603

Vestments Garments worn by Christian clergymen, colourful and richly decorated for Catholics

Key people

Anne Boleyn Henry VIII's second wife, who was executed in 1536 for adultery

Catherine of Aragon Henry VIII's first wife and the daughter of the King and Queen of Spain

Charles V Emperor who ruled Spain and the Holy Roman Empire from 1519 until 1556

Edward VI The only son of Henry VIII, he died aged fifteen and is known as the 'Boy King'

Henry VIII King of England from 1509 to 1547 who had six wives and started the English Reformation

Martin Luther A German monk and theologian who helped to start the Reformation

Thomas Cromwell Henry VIII's chief minister from 1532, and a strong Protestant

Thomas More Henry VIII's Lord Chancellor from 1529, he was executed for his Catholicism

Thomas Wolsey Henry VIII's Lord Chancellor from 1515 to 1529, and a very wealthy and powerful man

Mary I's Counter-reformation

During Edward VI's reign, his older sister Mary clung to her Roman Catholic faith.

Portrait of Mary I

She still attended Catholic mass in her private chapel even though it had been ruled illegal by her brother. When Edward told Mary off for this during a Christmas family dinner, she broke down in tears, asking Edward to kill her before he forced her to give up her Catholic faith.

On his deathbed, Edward VI ruled that his Protestant cousin Lady Jane Grey should be his heir. However, the great majority of England's population thought that their rightful Queen was Edward's half-sister Mary, and an army of around 20 000 men gathered to support her. After just nine days, Lady Jane Grey gave up her claim to the throne, and was locked in the Tower of London, forever to be remembered as the 'nine-days queen'. Mary became queen in July 1553, the first undisputed female monarch to rule England.

Marriage and rebellion

After Henry VIII had divorced Mary's mother, Catherine of Aragon, the 17-year-old Mary was ignored by her father and banned from seeing her mother. To make matters worse, Anne Boleyn soon gave Mary a Protestant half-sister called Elizabeth, whom Henry favoured. As Mary became more bitter and resentful, her attachment to Catholicism grew.

To prevent Elizabeth from succeeding her as Queen, Mary desperately needed to produce an heir. Mary intended to marry Philip II of Spain, the son of the Holy Roman Emperor Charles V. Philip was determined to defend the Catholic faith against the spread of Protestantism – a movement known as the **counter-reformation**.

Portrait of Philip II of Spain

A Catholic Spaniard was set to become king of England, and for many this was too much to bear. A knight called Sir Thomas Wyatt led a rebellion against Mary, but was defeated and captured in February 1554. Mary responded brutally: 120 rebels were hanged, and their bodies left to rot on the gallows in their home villages as a warning to others. Mary imprisoned her sister Elizabeth in the Tower of London, and executed her cousin Lady Jane Grey.

The Wyatt rebellion was a turning point in Mary's religious policy. In July 1554 she married Phillip, and confident that she would have an heir, Mary set about achieving a wholesale return of Catholicism to England.

'Bloody' Mary

Twenty years of religious reforms were put into reverse: churches were ordered to celebrate Mass and hold services in Latin; *The Book of Common Prayer* was outlawed; and priests who had married were forced to give up their wives. In November 1554, the heresy laws returned, and Protestants were once again burned at the stake.

> **Fact**
>
> In the last year of her life, Mary had a pain and a large lump in her stomach. She was convinced it was a child, but it was in fact the tumour that killed her.

English monarchs had used **burning at the stake** to punish heretics since the 1400s, but none used it quite as much as Mary. It was an agonisingly slow death, during which victims could feel, see and smell their flesh burn right before their eyes, suffering up to an hour of torturous pain before they died. Some witnesses reported seeing victims' blood boiling and steam bursting through the veins of their bodies.

In all, Mary had 283 Protestants burned at the stake, including 56 women, in five years. The most famous victim was Thomas Cranmer, the former Archbishop of Canterbury. Cranmer was England's leading Protestant and had masterminded Henry VIII's divorce from Catherine of Aragon. This had made Mary's teenage years a misery. Even though Cranmer renounced his Protestant faith six times, Mary still had him burned.

Mary suffered a number of miscarriages, and never bore an heir. Her husband Philip abandoned her and returned to Spain. On 17 November 1558, Mary died. To her Catholic supporters, she was remembered as 'Mary the Pious', but to her Protestant opponents she would always be remembered as 'Bloody Mary'.

Illustration of William Sautre being burned at the stake for heresy

Foxe's Book of Martyrs

John Foxe was a Protestant cleric who fled to Switzerland during Mary's reign. He wrote a bestselling account of the period in 1563. It was a powerful work of Protestant **propaganda**, which helped to establish Mary's reputation as 'Bloody'.

The book tells in vivid detail how each Protestant **martyr** died. One account describes the burning at the stake of two bishops, Latimer and Ridley. Friends of the two bishops tied bags of gunpowder around their necks to ensure a quick death, but the wet wood burned too slowly. Latimer was heard calling out to his dying friend, 'We shall this day light such a candle as I trust shall never be put out.'

Execution of the Duke of Suffolk, from Foxe's book

Check your understanding

1. How were Mary I's religious views different from those of her half-brother Edward VI?
2. Why did the Wyatt rebellion take place in 1554?
3. Why did Mary I's religious policy become more pro-Catholic, and anti-Protestant, from July 1554 onwards?
4. Why was being 'burned at the stake' such an agonising death?
5. What religious viewpoint was Foxe's Book of Martyrs written to support?

Unit 2: The later Tudors
Elizabeth I

In 1558, the throne passed to Mary's steely and independent-minded half-sister, Elizabeth I. She made a series of thoughtful decisions that would ensure the stability of her 44-year reign.

The most pressing issue facing Elizabeth was England's religion. In her lifetime, England had moved away from Catholicism and then back again under her father, much further towards Protestantism under her brother, and then back to Catholicism under her sister. When Elizabeth came to the throne, England was split between those Protestants who wanted to see the Reformation taken further, and those who still had a deep affection for Catholic ceremonies and rituals.

Elizabeth's religious policy, known as the '**Elizabethan Religious Settlement**', was a masterstroke of compromise. Elizabeth established a Church of England that was Protestant in doctrine, but Catholic in appearance. Cranmer's Book of Common Prayer returned, services were conducted in English, Catholic ceremonies and rituals were banned, and priests were allowed to marry. However, bishops were retained, priests could wear traditional vestments, and church decorations such as stained glass windows were permitted.

At first, Catholics were not forced to convert to Protestantism. Attendance at Protestant services on Sunday was compulsory, but the punishment for not attending was kept low: a fine of 12 pence. Elizabeth was willing to overlook Catholics who worshipped in private. As her advisor Sir Francis Bacon explained, she was not interested in creating 'windows into men's souls'.

Portrait of Elizabeth I

Marriage

The next challenge was marriage. Elizabeth's Protestant advisors, such as her loyal Secretary of State William Cecil, were desperate for Elizabeth to marry and produce an heir. An endless supply of English noblemen and European princes wanted Elizabeth's hand in marriage, but none was quite right.

Marrying a European royal such as Philip II of Spain or Prince Eric XIV of Sweden would have made England overly attached to a foreign power. Marrying an Englishman such as Robert Dudley, the Earl of Leicester, would have caused jealousy and conflict at home.

Though none of her advisors agreed with her, Elizabeth believed that she could serve England best by providing a long period of stability but no heir. Elizabeth's stubborn determination won out. As she told her court favourite Robert Dudley: "I will have here but one mistress and no master".

> **Fact**
>
> In 1558, the Scottish Protestant John Knox wrote a pamphlet expressing his outrage that women sat on both the English and Scottish thrones. Entitled *The first blast of the trumpet against the monstrous regiment of women,* his pamphlet argued that the natural order of society – by order of God's creation – was for men to dominate women.

Mary Queen of Scots

In 1570, the Pope issued a **Papal Bull** against the 'pretended Queen of England', declaring Elizabeth to be a heretic. It ordered English Catholics not to follow their queen, or risk being expelled from the Catholic Church.

Some English Catholics were driven to plot to kill the Queen, assured that this was the right path in the eyes of God. Elizabeth's government was thrown into panic. The greatest threat to Elizabeth was her Catholic younger cousin, Mary Queen of Scots (not to be confused with her half-sister Mary I). In 1568, Mary Queen of Scots was expelled from Scotland, and sought protection in England. Elizabeth was duty bound to offer shelter to her cousin, but Elizabeth also knew that some Catholics intended to kill her and place Mary Queen of Scots on the throne. So, for years Elizabeth imprisoned her cousin Mary in various **stately homes** and castles across England.

Portrait of Mary Queen of Scots

Elizabeth's government uncovered numerous Catholic plots to kill the queen, including one involving her own court doctor! After years of trying, Elizabeth's chief spymaster Francis Walsingham finally found the evidence he needed to implicate Mary. She had been communicating with a Catholic named Sir Anthony Babington who planned to assassinate Elizabeth I. They used coded letters, smuggled in and out of her prison in a waterproof case at the bottom of barrels, which Walsingham's spies managed to decode. In 1587, after 19 years of imprisonment, Mary Queen of Scots was beheaded.

As more and more plots against her life were uncovered, Elizabeth became increasingly intolerant towards Catholics. Fines for non-attendance at church increased, and in 1585 being a Catholic priest in England was made a crime punishable by death. In all, 180 Catholics were killed during Elizabeth's reign.

Fact

In many stately homes today, you can still see 'priest holes', where Catholic families would hide visiting priests, sometimes for days on end.

Francis Walsingham

Walsingham was Queen Elizabeth's chief 'spymaster', and had a network of spies across Europe. Walsingham would torture captured Catholics for further information. The Catholic priest Edmund Campion had iron spikes driven under his finger and toenails, and was placed on the **rack**. A Catholic from York named Margaret Clitherow was tortured by having a door put on top of her, and heavier and heavier weights were placed on the door until she died.

Check your understanding

1. What aspects of Catholicism did the Protestant Church of England retain under Elizabeth I?
2. Why did Elizabeth I believe neither a foreign nor an English husband would be suitable for her?
3. Why did the 1570 Papal Bull cause Elizabeth I's life to be in further danger?
4. What led to Mary Queen of Scots finally being sentenced to death in 1587?
5. How did Elizabeth I's treatment of Catholics in England change over the course of her reign?

The Elizabethan Golden Age

Due to Elizabeth I's wise decision making, England enjoyed an unprecedented period of peace and stability during her reign.

Art, trade and culture all flourished in England, and this period is sometimes termed the 'Elizabethan **Golden Age**'. Religious plays had been a strong part of the Catholic Church, but they were banned during the English Reformation. As a result, secular theatre became increasingly popular. Wealthy nobles would hire troupes of travelling actors to provide them with entertainment.

The theatre

In 1576, London gained its first public theatre. Built in the London suburb of Shoreditch and called The Theatre, it lay safely outside the city of London, where theatre had been banned. Theatre was very different during the Elizabethan period, with drinks and food sold in the stalls, and plenty of interaction between the actors and the audience. Rowdy audiences would cheer, boo and pelt poor performers with food. Elizabeth I enjoyed the theatre, and the best performances in London's public theatres would be transferred to perform at the royal court.

One of the few surviving portraits of William Shakespeare

There were many famous playwrights of this period, but none more so than William Shakespeare. Between 1590 and 1613, he wrote 38 plays including comedies such as *Much Ado About Nothing* and *A Midsummer Night's Dream*, tragedies such as *Hamlet* and *Macbeth*, and histories such as *Henry V* and *Richard III*. Little is known about Shakespeare's life, but he is thought to have gone to a grammar school in Stratford-Upon-Avon, before going to London to work as an actor. Many phrases that we still use today originated with Shakespeare, such as 'vanished into thin air', 'tongue-tied' and 'the game is up'.

The Elizabethan court

The Queen's favourite noblemen and advisors together made up the royal court. They would stay together in the Queen's various palaces, and enjoy glittering entertainments, such as plays, dancing, jousting, hunting, banqueting and concerts. Elizabeth I liked to surround herself with brilliant and handsome young men, such as Sir Walter Raleigh.

Raleigh was a dashing soldier, who had fought for the Protestants in France (known as Huguenots) during the **Wars of Religion**. He was 6 foot tall, had dark curly hair, and wore a pearl earring in one ear. In 1584, Queen Elizabeth asked him to build a colony in North America. He hosted two indigenous Americans named Manteo and Wanchese at his London home in an effort to learn their language, and made smoking American tobacco a fashionable pastime in Elizabeth's Court. Sir Walter Raleigh entranced Elizabeth with his charm, and many suspected Elizabeth

Portrait of Sir Walter Raleigh

was in love with him. When Elizabeth discovered that Raleigh had secretly married, she flew into a jealous rage and threw him in jail.

During the summer, Elizabeth would embark on her magnificent '**Royal progresses**', being hosted by members of her royal court across England. Favourites who wanted to impress the Queen spared no expense entertaining her at their stately homes, such as William Cecil's Burghley House.

Gloriana

By 1601, Queen Elizabeth was growing old. She was called to Parliament that year, as many of its members were angry with the high taxes needed to pay for war with Ireland. Elizabeth quelled their anger by delivering what became known as her 'Golden Speech'. It concluded: "And though you have had, and may have, many mightier and wiser princes sitting in this seat, yet you never had, nor shall have, any that will love you better."

Illustration of Queen Elizabeth I in procession with her courtiers

Aware that it was probably the last time they would hear their queen speak, the Members of Parliament lined up to kiss Elizabeth's hand as they left, many in tears. Two years later, Elizabeth died. After decades of religious conflict, she brought peace to England. Today, Elizabeth is remembered as one of England's greatest rulers.

Sir Francis Drake

Francis Drake has often been described as the greatest explorer of Elizabethan England. A tough young sailor from Devon, Drake began his career as a sea captain and slave trader. He worked for Queen Elizabeth as a '**privateer**', raiding Spanish **galleons** and trade ports in the Americas and returning to England with their cargo.

In an epic journey from 1577 to 1580, Drake became the first Englishman to circumnavigate the globe on his ship the *Golden Hind*. Having sailed through the treacherous Magellan Strait, Drake captured an unprotected Spanish galleon full of gold off the coast of Peru. When he returned from his voyage, Drake moored the *Golden Hind* in Deptford, and invited the Queen to join him for dinner on board. Elizabeth knighted Francis Drake on board the deck of his own ship.

Fact

In one famous story, Sir Walter Raleigh saved Elizabeth I from walking through a muddy puddle by throwing down his cape so that she could walk over it.

Check your understanding

1. Why did the theatre become increasingly popular during Elizabeth I's reign?
2. How was the theatre different during the Tudor period compared with the theatre today?
3. What were Queen Elizabeth's 'progresses'?
4. In what ways were Sir Walter Raleigh and Sir Francis Drake similar?
5. What did Elizabeth I tell the Members of Parliament during her Golden Speech?

The Spanish Armada

During Elizabeth I's reign, Philip II of Spain was the most powerful king in Europe. He was a leading defender of Catholicism in the European Wars of Religion.

As a devout Catholic, Philip II had many reasons to dislike England. He had briefly been King of England until the death of Mary I. Philip courted Elizabeth I as his next wife, but Elizabeth rejected Philip's advances. Elizabeth gave English support to Protestant armies fighting in Europe, and she openly ordered English privateers such as Francis Drake to attack and rob Spanish ships of their precious cargo whilst returning from the Americas.

When Elizabeth executed Mary Queen of Scots in 1587, this seemed to guarantee a Protestant future for England. Philip II knew he would have to act fast if England was to return to the old faith.

The Armada

Philip set about building the largest naval invasion force Europe had ever seen. On 28 May 1588, it set sail from Lisbon for England. Named the 'Spanish **Armada**', Philip's force consisted of 130 large ships known as 'galleons', 8000 sailors and 18 000 soldiers. However, it had one crucial weakness: the commander of the fleet, the Duke of Medina Sidonia, had little sailing experience. He even suffered from seasickness.

In Holland, the Spanish had a crack-force of 30 000 experienced soldiers under the command of the Duke of Parma. Philip's plan was for the Armada to sail to France where he would meet the Duke of Parma's army, and then invade England. The English navy, under the command of Lord Howard of Effingham and Francis Drake, numbered 200 ships. Though more numerous, their ships were smaller, and had much less gun-power.

After weeks of waiting, the Spanish Armada was sighted off the coast of Cornwall on 19 July. A series of hilltop bonfires called 'signalling towers' were lit. This spread the news towards London and across the south coast: England was under attack.

That evening, the Spanish approached the English fleet moored in Plymouth. With the wind blowing into the harbour, the English were vulnerable to attack, and the Spanish had their best chance of a quick and easy victory. However, Medina Sidonia wanted to stick to his orders to meet the Duke of Parma in France first, so he sailed straight past the English fleet.

Painting of English and Spanish ships during the Armada, completed shortly after the event

For a week, the English chased the Spanish up the channel, engaging in a few skirmishes. Then, on the 27 July, the Spanish anchored off Calais to pick up their reinforcements. To their shock, the Duke of Parma had not yet arrived. His army of 30 000 men was nowhere to be seen.

English victory

The following evening, on the 28 July, the English devised a tactical masterstroke. They filled eight ships with gunpowder and tar, creating '**hellburners**'. In the middle of the night, these were set on a course for the Spanish ships anchored at Calais. The Spanish commanders awoke to see the burning ships speeding towards them, and panicked. They cut their anchors and were scattered along the channel.

Modern illustration of the English hellburners

As a consequence, the Spanish lost their powerful 'crescent' formation, and were easy to attack. On the 7 August, the two sides met at the Battle of Gravelines, where the smaller English ships sailed rings around the larger Spanish galleons, sinking five and damaging many more.

At this point, Medina Sidonia made a serious navigational error, and the Armada was blown north towards Scotland. They then had to sail past Scotland and down the west coast of Ireland to safety, but were caught in treacherous storms. Around 60 Spanish ships were wrecked on the Scottish and Irish coasts, and 11 000 Spanish soldiers died. It is sometimes claimed that people living on the west coast of Ireland today are descended from Spanish sailors who were shipwrecked during the Armada.

Tilbury speech

The day after the Battle of Gravelines, Elizabeth I visited her troops who were stationed at Tilbury and awaiting the invasion. Dressed in a silver suit of armour, Elizabeth delivered the most famous speech of her reign. In it she declared: *"I know I have the body of a weak and feeble woman; but I have the heart and stomach of a king – and of a King of England too."*

Little did Elizabeth know, the English Royal Navy had already defeated the Spanish Armada. Had they not, Philip II may well have deposed Elizabeth I, and returned England to Catholicism. The history of England could have been very different indeed.

Fact

A year before the Armada, Francis Drake made a first strike on the Spanish fleet harboured in the Spanish port of Cadiz. Drake took them by surprise, sank 30 ships and set fire to the city. The Spanish gave him the nickname 'El Draque', meaning 'the dragon'.

Check your understanding

1. Why did Philip II of Spain want to invade England?

2. Why was it such a mistake for Medina Sidonia not to attack on the evening of 19th July?

3. Why did the English send 'hellburners' sailing towards the Spanish ships moored in Calais?

4. What happened to the Spanish Armada following the Battle of Gravelines?

5. What message did Elizabeth I deliver to the troops in her Tilbury Speech?

Rich and poor in Tudor England

By the time the Tudors came to power, some of England's most powerful noble families had died out during the Wars of the Roses.

Fewer noblemen meant fewer challenges to the monarchy, and the Tudor monarchs made sure that the nobility remained small and easily managed for the rest of their reigns.

When the Catholic Duke of Norfolk was executed in 1572 for treason, there were no more dukes left in England. By 1600, there was one marquess, 18 earls, two viscounts and 37 barons, making up a class of just 58 noblemen in the whole country. Most significantly, starting with the reign of Henry VII, it was illegal for noblemen to keep private armies. Many swapped their now unnecessary castles for stately homes. Tudor noblemen were still great landowners, but their days as an elite military class were over.

The gentry

The real ruling class of Tudor England was the **gentry**. Numbering around 15 000 families, members of the gentry were landowners without noble titles. Like the nobility, they made enough money from renting their land to tenant farmers to pursue lives of leisure. The gentry had the time to read and socialise, and called themselves 'gentlemen'.

Painting of a fair in Bermondsey, near London, from 1569

The decreasing power of the nobility during the Tudor period made it surprisingly easy for bright men of humble birth to rise to the top of society, as can be seen in the careers of Thomas Wolsey and Thomas Cromwell. Called '**new men**', many of these upwardly mobile Tudors benefited from the Dissolution of the Monasteries. It allowed them to buy church land cheaply and become landowning gentlemen.

The division between the landed wealthy and the working poor were as clear as ever in Tudor England. The medieval Sumptuary Laws remained in place, so only a nobleman could wear gold or silver cloth, and only a lord could wear red or blue velvet. At the other end of the scale, the Wool Cap Act of 1571 stated that all working people over the age of seven had to wear a wool cap on Sundays or holy days.

For the wealthy, fashions in Tudor England were always changing. During the reign of Elizabeth I, men began to wear short padded trousers called **hose**, and a buttoned up jacket known as a **doublet**. Women wore stiff bodices that were tightened to make their waists look small, and a wide hoop structure for their dresses called a **farthingale**. This allowed them to display

Painting of the diplomat Sir Henry Unton, with a rather large ruff

their expensive fabric, embellished with jewels, ribbons and lace. Women also put white powder on their face and plucked their hairlines back. From the 1560s onwards, any self-respecting lady or **gentleman** had to wear a **ruff**: an elaborate lace collar encircling the neck, which – as the playwright Ben Johnson observed – created the impression of a head on a plate.

Life for the poor

The population of England grew rapidly during this period, almost doubling from 2.4 million in 1520 to 4.1 million in 1600. This meant there were often not enough jobs to go round, so mass unemployment was common. To make matters worse, England's monasteries – which for centuries had cared for the poor during times of hardship – no longer existed.

Tudor woodcut showing a vagrant being whipped through the streets

As a result, travelling beggars called **vagrants** became a common sight in Tudor towns, and people in Tudor England often spoke of an increase in crime. At first, Tudor governments responded harshly. Begging was made illegal for everyone except elderly people or people with disabilities. Able-bodied vagrants caught begging would have a large hole burnt through their right ear with a hot iron. If they reoffended, vagrants could be imprisoned or even executed.

The government did gradually begin to take more responsibility for the poor. From 1563 onwards, the '**Poor Laws**' were passed, requiring parishes to collect taxes from the local population, to provide help for the poor. The Tudors made a clear distinction between two different types of poor. The **'deserving' poor**, who were unable to work through old age, disability or the lack of jobs, were believed to deserve help. Whereas it was believed the 'undeserving' poor were simply idle, and deserved nothing.

Tudor football

Sport was very popular in Tudor England, in particular football. Aside from being played with a leather ball, there were few similarities with the modern game. Tudor football was often played between villages, with no boundaries to the pitch, and no limit to the number of players on each side. Players could pick up and run with the ball. Fights, broken bones, and even deaths were common.

Fact

Elizabeth I was no exception to the Tudor love of fashion. An inventory of the royal wardrobe in 1600 recorded that she owned 269 gowns, 96 cloaks, and 99 robes.

Check your understanding

1. Why was the nobility weaker during the Tudor period, than in the medieval period?
2. Why were landowners such as the nobility and gentry able to pursue lives of leisure?
3. How did men's fashions change from the reign of Henry VIII, to the reign of Elizabeth I?
4. Why was vagrancy such a problem during the 16th century?
5. What was the difference, according to the Poor Laws, between the deserving and the undeserving poor?

Unit 2: The later Tudors
Knowledge organiser

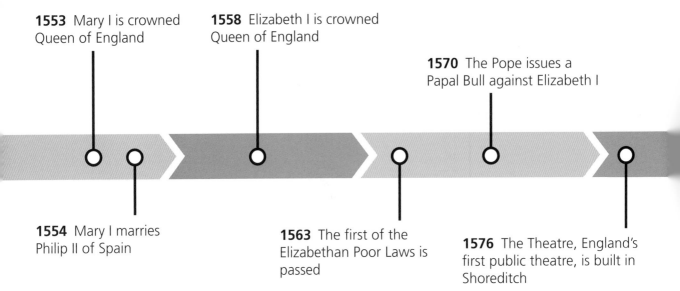

1553 Mary I is crowned Queen of England

1558 Elizabeth I is crowned Queen of England

1570 The Pope issues a Papal Bull against Elizabeth I

1554 Mary I marries Philip II of Spain

1563 The first of the Elizabethan Poor Laws is passed

1576 The Theatre, England's first public theatre, is built in Shoreditch

Key vocabulary

Armada Fleet of warships, often used to describe Spanish force sent to invade England in 1588

Babington Plot A foiled plot to kill Elizabeth I, which resulted in Mary Queen of Scots' execution

Burning at the stake A slow and painful execution, usually reserved for religious heretics

Counter-reformation Catholic fightback against the spread of Protestantism in Europe

Deserving poor Category developed by the Tudors for those amongst the poor in genuine need of help

Doublet and hose A buttoned up jacket and short padded trousers worn during the Tudor period

Elizabethan Religious Settlement A compromise agreement returning England to Protestantism but allowing Catholics to worship in secret

Farthingale A wide hoop structure worn beneath a dress, in order to display expensive fabrics and decorations

Foxe's Book of Martyrs A work of Protestant propaganda against Mary I, published in 1563

Galleon A large sailing ship, particularly from Spain

Gentleman Someone who earns enough money from land and investments not to work for a living

Gentry Class of wealthy landowners without noble titles, positioned just below the nobility

Gloriana A name given to Elizabeth towards the end of her reign, from the Latin for 'glorious'

Golden Age A period of flourishing in the history of a nation or an art form

Golden Hind Sir Francis Drake's ship, on which he completed his circumnavigation of the world

Hellburner A ship filled with explosives, set alight, abandoned and sailed towards the enemy

Martyr A person who is killed for their beliefs, often religious

New men Upwardly mobile men of the Tudor period, who benefitted from the weakening nobility

Papal Bull A formal and important announcement, issued by the Pope

Poor Laws Laws passed during the Tudor period, making local parishes raise money to help the poor

Privateer A private sailor or pirate, authorised by their government to attack enemy ships

Propaganda A piece of art or information used to promote a particular cause or point of view

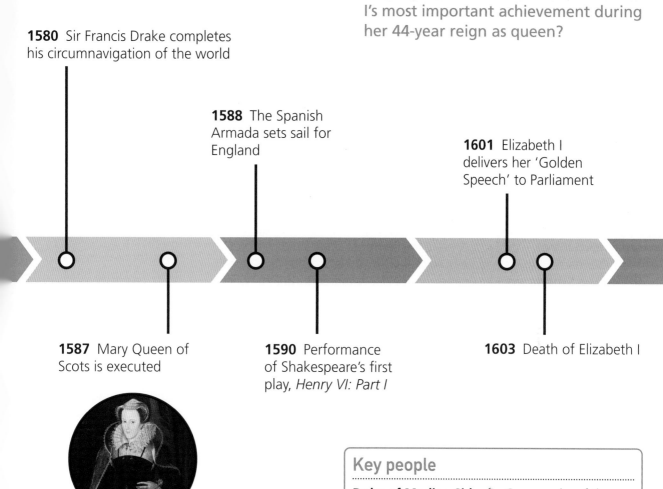

1580 Sir Francis Drake completes his circumnavigation of the world

1588 The Spanish Armada sets sail for England

1601 Elizabeth I delivers her 'Golden Speech' to Parliament

1587 Mary Queen of Scots is executed

1590 Performance of Shakespeare's first play, *Henry VI: Part I*

1603 Death of Elizabeth I

Key vocabulary

Rack Torture device used slowly to stretch a person's body until all their joints dislocate

Royal Progress A summer journey taken by a monarch, visiting the stately homes of court favourites

Ruff An elaborate lace collar encircling the neck, fashionable during the Elizabethan period

Stately home A large country house at the centre of a gentleman or a noble's estate

Vagrant A person with no job, who travels from place to place begging

Wars of Religion A series of European wars fought between Protestants and Catholics from 1524 to 1648

Key people

Duke of Medina Sidonia Commander of the Spanish Armada, who suffered from seasickness

Elizabeth I Queen from 1558 to 1603, and remembered as one of England's greatest monarchs

Francis Walsingham Principal Secretary and 'spymaster' to Elizabeth I

Lady Jane Grey Cousin of Edward VI, known as the 'nine-days Queen' for her very brief reign

Mary I Queen who led England's counter-reformation, and earned the epithet 'Bloody'

Mary Queen of Scots Elizabeth I's Catholic cousin and the most significant threat to her reign

Philip II of Spain King of Spain, who for a time was the husband of Mary I and King of England

Francis Drake Sailor and privateer, and the first Englishman to circumnavigate the globe

Walter Raleigh English sailor and explorer, and a noted favourite of Queen Elizabeth I

William Shakespeare Celebrated English playwright who worked during the Tudor and Stuart periods

Unit 3: The English Civil War
James I and the Gunpowder Plot

Queen Elizabeth I died in 1603 leaving no direct heir to the throne. Her successor was to be found in Scotland, where the Protestant James VI was king.

James VI was the great-great-grandson of the first Tudor king, Henry VII, and the son of Mary Queen of Scots. In 1603, the 36-year-old King of Scotland became James I of England. His coronation in London united England and Scotland under the same monarch, but they were still two separate countries, with two separate **Parliaments**. James did not keep the Tudor name, but instead he used the name of his Scottish royal family: Stuart. The **Stuarts** would rule England for one hundred turbulent, war-torn years.

James's religion

People did not know what religious policy James I would pursue. His mother Mary was a Catholic martyr, but Mary had been imprisoned when James was just one year old. James was then brought up as a strict Protestant by his tutors. When James I came to the throne, English Catholics hoped that their new king would pursue a policy of **religious toleration** for Catholics. James's advisors, in particular his strongly Protestant Secretary of State Robert Cecil, made sure this was not the case.

Elizabeth I's anti-Catholic laws stayed in place: Catholic priests could be executed; dying Catholics could not be offered last rites; Catholics could not go to university; and Catholics who avoided Protestant church on Sundays would be fined £20 – an enormous sum of money at the time. By 1605, some English Catholics were desperate. They believed that only extreme action could ever return England to the old faith.

> **Fact**
>
> A significant landmark of James's reign was his authorisation of the King James Bible, which translated both the Old and the New Testament into English. Completed in 1611, it remains the most widely published book in the English language to this day. James also wrote *Daemonologie* which was extensively used during the witch trials that escalated during and after his reign.

The Gunpowder Plot

If it had been successful, the Gunpowder Plot would have been the most destructive terrorist attack in English history. Robert Catesby masterminded the plot, assembling a group of 12 Catholic plotters. The group included a battle-hardened soldier from York called Guy Fawkes. For 10 years Fawkes had fought as a mercenary for the Spanish Catholics against Dutch Protestants in the Wars of Religion, so was given responsibility for the explosives.

Contemporary engraving of the gunpowder plotters

Another plotter rented a cellar beneath the Houses of Parliament from a government official. Guy Fawkes packed the cellar with 36 barrels of gunpowder. The plan was to light the fuse on the morning of 5 November 1605. This was the same day as the **state opening of Parliament**, and the royal family, the royal court and both houses of Parliament would all have been present. The explosion would have killed off most of England's ruling class, after which the plotters planned to put James I's daughter Princess Elizabeth on the throne as a puppet queen.

The letter

However, one of the plotters, named Francis Tresham, was worried that his brother-in-law Lord Monteagle would be at the state opening of Parliament. Tresham sent Lord Monteagle an anonymous letter telling him to think up an excuse not to attend Parliament that day, hinting that those who did attend "shall receive a terrible blow this Parliament and yet they shall not see who hurts them". On receiving the letter on 26 October, Lord Monteagle was suspicious, and immediately took it to Robert Cecil. Cecil waited until the morning of 5 November to act, when he sent the king's troops to search the cellars below Parliament.

FAC-SIMILE OF THE LETTER WRITTEN TO LORD MONTEAGLE
WHICH LED TO THE DISCOVERY OF THE GUNPOWDER PLOT.

Copy of the letter sent from Tresham to his brother-in-law Lord Monteagle

Here, Guy Fawkes was caught red-handed preparing to light the gunpowder fuse. Fawkes was seized, and tortured on the rack. After four days of agonising pain he confessed to his crime, and gave away the names of his fellow plotters. They were quickly tracked down by the king's men to a stately home in Staffordshire. Some were shot and killed whilst resisting arrest, and the surviving plotters were brought back to London where they were tried for **treason**. The plotters were hanged, drawn and quartered, with their hearts and intestines removed and burnt in front of them. Their heads were placed on spikes by London Bridge.

After such a close brush with death, any policy of toleration for Catholics in England was unthinkable for Parliament and the king. Anti-Catholic laws were strengthened. When Members of Parliament finally met, they instituted a 'public thanksgiving to almighty God every year on the fifth day of November'. This annual event took the form of bonfires, on which effigies of Guy Fawkes were burnt, giving birth to the English tradition of Bonfire Night.

Modern illustration of Guy Fawkes in the cellar below Parliament

Check your understanding

1. Why were England and Scotland ruled by the same king following the death of Elizabeth I?
2. Why were English Catholics particularly frustrated by James I's religious policy?
3. Why did the Gunpowder Plotters choose 5 November as the date to blow up Parliament?
4. How did Robert Cecil come to find out about the Gunpowder Plot?
5. What were the consequences, in terms of religious policy, of the Gunpowder Plot?

Charles I and Parliament

Since at least the days of Magna Carta, most English monarchs had accepted that they should share power with the people they ruled.

However, coming from Scotland, the Stuart kings thought differently. The Stuarts believed that because God was all-powerful, their family must have been chosen to rule England directly by God. To question them, therefore was to question God. This belief was called the '**Divine Right of Kings**'. King of Scotland, James I wrote a book called *The True Law of Free Monarchies*, which explained: "Kings are called Gods; they are appointed by God and answerable only to God".

Engraving of Charles I illustrating the Divine Right of Kings

Charles I

James I's son Charles was a shy and sickly child, who only learned to walk and talk at the age of four, and suffered from a stammer that would stay with him his entire life. He was crowned Charles I after the death of his father in 1625, and showed a fatal combination of bad judgement and stubbornness.

The early years of Charles I's reign were a catalogue of errors. In order to make peace with France, he married the daughter of the King of France, a Catholic named Henrietta Maria. War with France continued anyway, and many of England's Protestant population were now furious their king was married to a foreign Catholic.

Some even suspected Charles was a secret Catholic, who planned for the old faith to creep back into the Church of England. These suspicions increased when he appointed William Laud as Archbishop of Canterbury in 1633. Laud brought many aspects of Catholic services back into the Church of England, and sent inspectors to parishes across the country who would fine any priests not following his reforms. This disturbed the overwhelmingly Protestant people of England: it has been estimated by this time 97 per cent of England's population were Protestant, as were 88 per cent of the nobility and gentry.

> ### Fact
>
> To demonstrate their divine power, Stuart kings continued a medieval practice known as '**touching for the king's evil**'. This involved touching people with a skin disease called scrofula in order to heal them.

Most concerned by Charles's sympathy for Catholicism were England's **Puritans** (see box). Many Puritans sat in Parliament, where they repeatedly questioned Charles I's policies and tried to limit his power. By 1629, Charles was sick of Parliament questioning his divine right to rule. So, from 1629 until 1640 Charles ruled without calling Parliament once, a period known as the '**eleven-years tyranny**'. Charles wanted to be like the **absolutist** monarchs of Europe, such as the powerful Catholic Kings of France, Louis XIII and XIV.

Charles I and his Catholic wife Henrietta Maria

However, without Parliament, Charles had no means of raising new taxes. He found a clever way around this problem. There was an old tax called '**ship money**', which was used to tax towns by the coast and build up the navy when England was under threat of invasion (such as during the Spanish Armada). Charles did not need Parliament's permission to raise ship money so, even though England was at peace, he extended it to all parts of the country. Soon, ship money was making Charles £200 000 a year, and he spent the money on anything but ships: in particular his fine clothing, new palaces and enormous art collection.

In 1637 John Hampden, a wealthy landowner and **Member of Parliament** (MP), was imprisoned for refusing to pay ship money, and became a hero for Parliament's cause. Those who criticised Charles I could be called before his own personal court, the **Star Chamber**. When a Puritan lawyer called William Prynne published a book in 1632 which implied the king's dances were immoral, he was put on trial before the Star Chamber. Prynne was imprisoned for life, and had his face branded and both his ears chopped off. Charles I, some believed, was becoming a tyrant.

Puritans

During the 1600s, a radical form of Protestantism became popular in England. Its followers tried to live lives that were as godly and 'pure' as possible, so became known as 'Puritans'.

Puritans wanted a world of strict Christianity, a 'heaven on earth' with no sin or wickedness. They wore simple black clothing, as they believed that jewellery, make up and colourful clothing were sinful. Activities such as gambling, drunkenness, dancing, music, theatre and sport were also frowned upon, and on Sundays no activity was allowed except for reading the Bible and going to church. Puritans did not believe the English Reformation had done enough to change the Church of England, and had a fierce dislike of Catholicism.

Portrait of a Puritan family from the 1640s by the Dutch artist Frans Hals

Because they were hard working, and did not spend much money, many Puritans became successful merchants and farmers. As they grew wealthier, Puritans gained more political power.

Check your understanding

1. What was meant by 'the Divine Right of Kings'?
2. What was misjudged about Charles I's decision to marry Henrietta Maria?
3. Why was the period between 1629 and 1640 known as the 'eleven-years tyranny'?
4. Why was Charles I's decision to collect taxation through ship money so controversial?
5. Why were England's Puritans gaining power during the Stuart period?

Unit 3: The English Civil War
The outbreak of war

From 1637 onwards, a series of events sent England tumbling towards **civil war**. It began with troubles north of the border, in Scotland.

The Reformation had been particularly strong in Scotland, where a form of Protestantism known as **Presbyterianism** had taken hold. From 1560, committees of clergymen and laymen ran the Church of Scotland, with no royally appointed bishops. James I and Charles I did manage to reintroduce some bishops to Scotland, but they did not have the power of English bishops.

To increase Charles I's power over the Church of Scotland, Archbishop Laud devised a new prayer book for Scotland, with some aspects of Catholic services. When Laud's prayer book was first used at St Giles Cathedral, Edinburgh in 1637, the Scottish congregation rioted. They threw wooden stools at the clergy, and accused them of 'popery'. Soon, there was an open rebellion against Charles I throughout Scotland, known as the **Bishops' War**. In 1640, a Scottish army marched across the border and occupied England as far south as Yorkshire.

The Long Parliament

Charles I urgently needed to raise an army and end the Bishops' War. However, for an army, he needed to raise new taxes, and to raise new taxes he needed Parliament. Charles recalled Parliament in April 1640, but dissolved it three weeks later after it refused to raise the money he needed for the Bishops' War. In September, Charles called Parliament again. This Parliament would remain in session, on and off, for the next 20 years. It became known as the '**Long Parliament**'.

Charles only expected Parliament to meet and approve new taxes. After 11 years of being ignored, however, Members of Parliament had a long list of demands for the king. They wanted to meet every three years; they wanted an end to ship money; and they did not want the king to have the power to dissolve Parliament without their permission. Some Puritan Members of the Long Parliament, such as the lawyer John Pym, went even further. They asked for Bishops to be removed from the Church of England; all of Henrietta Maria's Catholic friends to be expelled from court; and for the tutors of Charles I's son – the future King of England – to be chosen by them.

Parliament also wanted to punish some of Charles's closest advisors. Archbishop Laud was accused of treason, and imprisoned in the Tower of London. Another of the king's

Contemporary engraving of the execution of the Earl of Strafford

favourites, the Earl of Strafford, was accused of negotiating with an army in Ireland to invade England and suppress opposition to the king. Parliament sentenced Strafford to death for treason, and forced Charles I to sign his friend's death warrant.

Arguments raged for another year, but neither Parliament nor the king would give in. Urged on by his queen Henrietta Maria, Charles decided on 4 January 1642 to show his strength by arresting, in person, the five most troublesome Members of Parliament, including John Pym and John Hampden. It was a catastrophic error of judgement. Charles marched into Parliament, sat in the Speaker's Chair, and read out their names. However, the MPs had been tipped off in advance, and escaped down the River Thames. Charles looked round Parliament in despair, and observed, "I see all my birds have flown".

The failed arrest of the five members was a disaster for Charles. It made him seem both weak and tyrannical. Over the following days, the people of London became increasingly agitated, building barricades, collecting weapons, and attacking the houses of suspected Catholics.

Victorian painting of the failed arrest of the five Members of Parliament

War

Charles decided it was no longer safe for his family to stay in London. On 10 January 1642, he fled for York. Parliament was effectively left in charge of the country. In March, Parliament passed the '**Militia Ordinance**' stating that the army was under their control. War, it seemed, was inevitable.

Different parts of England started to declare for either the 'Royalist' or the 'Parliamentarian' side. On 22 August, Charles I raised the King's standard in Nottingham – showing his intention to fight Parliament. The English Civil War had begun.

Civil wars are uniquely horrific events. Towns and families are split apart, pitching fathers against sons, brothers against brothers, and friends against friends. One in four English men fought at some point during the English Civil War. Around 11 000 houses were burned or demolished, including historic stately houses such as Basing House and Corfe Castle. 150 towns saw serious damage, and an estimated 5 per cent of England's population died due to war or disease – a higher proportion than died during the First World War.

Fact

In 1641, Charles I travelled to Scotland to make peace with the leaders of the Bishops' War. Whilst there, he played a round of a popular Scottish sport called golf.

Check your understanding

1. What caused the Bishops' War to start in Scotland?
2. Why did the Bishops' War force Charles I to recall Parliament?
3. What sort of demands did Members of Parliament make once Parliament had been recalled?
4. Why was his attempt to arrest the five Members of Parliament such a catastrophe for Charles I?
5. What event marked the beginning of the English Civil War?

Unit 3: The English Civil War
Fighting the English Civil War

Having fled the city in January 1642, Charles I's primary objective at the beginning of the English Civil War was to retake London.

There were three major battles. The first conflict was at the Battle of Edgehill, just outside Warwickshire, in October 1642. The outcome of the battle was indecisive. When Charles I's weary army attempted to take London, it was repelled by local citizen militias called **trainbands** at Turnham Green.

The next major battle was at Marston Moor near York in July 1644. The war had been going the **Royalists'** way for two years, but at the Battle of Marston Moor the **Parliamentarians** won their first major victory against Charles. Prince Rupert's **cavalry** was routed – as Oliver Cromwell said, "God made them as stubble to our swords". After Marston Moor, the Parliamentarians gained control of northern England.

A year later in July 1645 the Parliamentarians delivered a killer blow to the Royalists at the Battle of Naseby near Leicester. Almost the entire Royalist army was killed or captured, and Parliament's troops seized the king's baggage train. Here, they found £100 000 in jewels and treasure, and the king's private correspondence.

Painting of Prince Rupert, the archetypal cavalier

Published later that year, Charles's letters showed he had been negotiating with Irish and French armies to invade England and put him back on the throne. In return, Charles had promised to repeal anti-Catholic laws. The king's enemies used this as evidence that Charles was planning treason against his own people, and they began to refer to him as 'Charles Stuart, that man of Blood'. After Naseby, Parliament seized the Royalist headquarters at Oxford. Charles I was left defeated and disgraced.

Cavalier

The Royalists, who fought for the king, were mostly recruited from the nobility, some Catholics, and people from the countryside. The Royalist cavalrymen were often of noble birth, and liked to have long hair and expensive clothing. They went into battle wearing knee high boots with high heels, colourful decorated tunics, soft leather gloves, shirts with ruffled cuffs, and beaver hats with ostrich feather plumes.

Like the knights of medieval Europe, Royalist cavalrymen saw themselves as romantic figures. They were nicknamed '**Cavaliers**' after the Spanish word 'caballero', meaning horseman. The archetypal cavalier was Prince Rupert, a nephew of Charles I, who travelled from Germany to England aged only 23 to command the Royalist cavalry.

> **Fact**
>
> Prince Rupert would take with him to battle his pet dog, a poodle called Boye, who some Roundheads believed had magical powers. Boye was captured and killed at the Battle of Marston Moor.

Prince Rupert was a flamboyant character. On the battlefield, he was a brave and skilled commander, but could get carried away. At the Battle of Edgehill, he chased the retreating Parliamentarian forces too far and lost his chance to win a real victory. At the Battle of Marston Moor, he was still having a dinner party with his officers when the Parliamentarians attacked.

Roundhead

The Parliamentarian soldiers were nicknamed '**Roundheads**', due to the shaved heads of some of Parliament's supporters. Parliamentarians were mostly recruited from minor gentry or people living in towns, many of whom were Puritans. They had a more disciplined approach to war than the Cavaliers. Whilst the Cavaliers spent the first winter of the war throwing expensive parties, the Parliamentarians trained their army.

In 1645, a Puritan cavalry general called Oliver Cromwell set about creating a full-time Parliamentarian army. Called the '**New Model Army**', they were strictly disciplined and devoted to Parliament's cause. Drinking and swearing were forbidden, and deserting was punished with public floggings. They were a professional army, with red uniforms, simple practical clothing, and metal armour. Cromwell's cavalry forces were so formidable, they were nicknamed the 'Ironsides'.

Modern illustration of Parliamentarian soldiers

Most importantly, the New Model Army believed they were fighting in a holy war. They would sing hymns marching into battle, and read from the Bible or listen to sermons that inspired them to fight. Promotion in the New Model Army was gained not through wealth or high-birth, but through merit. As Cromwell said: "I would rather have a plain russet-coated captain that knows what he fights for, and loves what he knows, than that which you call a gentleman and is nothing else."

Political radicals

During the turmoil of the Civil War, some people developed political ideas that were surprisingly radical for the 17th century. One group argued for equal legal and political rights for all men. They were called the '**Levellers**', as they wanted to level out the hierarchy of Stuart society. Another group, called the 'Diggers', established a religious community in Surrey with common ownership of all land and possessions.

Check your understanding

1. What was Charles I's main objective at the beginning of the English Civil War?
2. Why was Charles I left disgraced after the Battle of Naseby?
3. What was the character of Prince Rupert?
4. How did the approach of the Parliamentarian army differ from that of the Cavaliers?
5. How did the religious beliefs of the New Model Army influence their behaviour?

Trial and execution

After his defeat at the Battle of Naseby, Charles I surrendered to the Scots in April 1646. He believed the Scots would treat him better as a prisoner than Parliament would.

This marked the end of the first Civil War. In June, Parliament met with Charles I in Newcastle to discuss a peace settlement. Parliament put forward a set of demands, known as the **Newcastle Propositions** (see box), but Charles saw the demands as an insult. He refused them outright.

The Scots soon tired of holding Charles I as a prisoner, and sold him to Parliament for £400 000 in February 1647. The king was now Parliament's prisoner, but still they were unable to agree on a settlement. In November 1647, Charles I escaped from his prison in Hampton Court and rode south to the Isle of Wight. This sparked a second Civil War, and Royalist uprisings took place in Kent, Essex, Yorkshire, Wales and Cornwall. In addition, Charles I had secretly been negotiating with a Scottish army, who invaded England in support of the king. By September 1648, Parliament had won the second Civil War with a bloody three-day battle at Preston.

By now, the most extreme opponents to the king were not in Parliament, but in the army. The New Model Army had grown too large and powerful for Parliament to control, and when Parliament ordered the army to disband in 1646, it refused. Led by the Oliver Cromwell, the army began to argue that more radical action against Charles I was needed.

The Newcastle Propositions

Some of the demands were:

- The Church of England should no longer have bishops
- Royalist estates be handed over to Parliament
- Parliament should remain in control of the army for 20 years
- Parliament should choose membership of the king's government

Trial

On 5 December 1648, Parliament voted to continue negotiations with the king, but the army had other ideas. The following day, a soldier called Colonel Pride invaded Parliament, arresting 45 Members of Parliament for supporting the king, and expelling a further 186 for supporting further negotiations.

'**Pride's Purge**', as it became known, was a crucial turning point. Now just 200 strong opponents of Charles I remained as Members of Parliament, and many were ready to try him for treason. When Cromwell

Rapier, a lightweight sword used during the English Civil war

was told that it was legally impossible to try a king, he replied "I tell you we will cut off his head with his crown upon it!".

The trial of Charles I began on 20 January 1649, in Westminster Hall. Parliament was renamed the High Court of Justice, and Charles was tried for being "A tyrant, traitor, murderer and a public and implacable enemy to the commonwealth of England". The prosecution argued that Charles had begun the Civil War against his own people, and was therefore responsible for all of the death and destruction that followed. They also accused him of treason for conspiring with France and Ireland to invade England on his behalf.

Contemporary painting of the execution of Charles I by an unknown artist

Charles refused to answer the charges. He argued that because treason is defined as a crime against the king, it is impossible to try a king for treason. Even if Charles had defended himself, the verdict was not in question after Pride's Purge. The remaining MPs appointed 135 commissioners to act as judges, but even then only 59 signed Charles I's death warrant. The others stayed away through fear or disapproval.

Execution

Charles was led to the executioner's block on 30 January 1649. The execution took place outside **Banqueting House**, a beautifully ornate part of the Palace of Whitehall built by Charles and his father James. The day was bitterly cold, and Charles asked to wear two shirts, so that he did not appear to be shivering with fear. Before his execution Charles declared, "I go from a corruptible to an incorruptible crown".

With one strike of the axe, his head was chopped off. There was a deathly silence, before soldiers began to disperse the spectators in order to avoid a riot. Many members of the crowd dipped their handkerchiefs in the king's blood, believing that it would have divine powers.

The crowd could not quite believe what they had seen. Due to the army's radicalisation, Charles I had been executed against the will of the great majority of England's population. It was as if England had become a republic by accident.

Fact

The chief judge at the trial of Charles I, John Bradshaw, was so worried about the threat to his life that he wore a beaver hat lined with steel and a suit of armour beneath his clothes.

Judge Bradshaw's steel-lined hat

Check your understanding

1. Why did Charles I refuse to agree to the Newcastle Propositions?
2. Why were Parliamentarians quickly losing patience with Charles I by September 1648?
3. On what grounds did Parliament try Charles I for treason in 1649?
4. Why did Charles I refuse to answer any of the charges during his trial?
5. What was the response of the London crowd to the execution of Charles I?

Unit 3: The English Civil War
Knowledge organiser

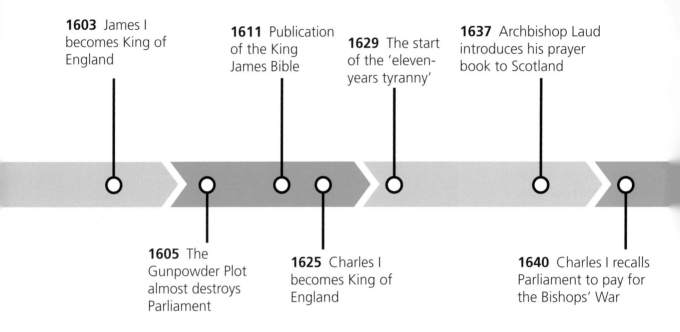

1603 James I becomes King of England

1611 Publication of the King James Bible

1629 The start of the 'eleven-years tyranny'

1637 Archbishop Laud introduces his prayer book to Scotland

1605 The Gunpowder Plot almost destroys Parliament

1625 Charles I becomes King of England

1640 Charles I recalls Parliament to pay for the Bishops' War

---

Key vocabulary

Absolutist A ruler who has absolute power over his or her people

Banqueting House Ornate building in the Palace of Whitehall outside which Charles I was executed

Bishops' War An uprising against Charles I's religious reforms which began in Scotland

Cavalier The nickname for Royalist cavalrymen during the English Civil War

Cavalry Soldiers mounted on horseback

Civil War A war between two sides from the same nation

Divine Right of Kings The theory that a monarch is appointed by God and should have absolute power

Levellers A radical group during the Civil War who demanded equal legal and political rights

Long Parliament A Parliament which met, on and off, from 1640 to 1660

Member of Parliament Someone elected to sit in the House of Commons, often abbreviated to 'MP'

Militia Ordinance A law by which the English Parliament took control of the army from Charles I

Newcastle Propositions A series of demands devised by Parliament in 1646, and rejected by Charles I

New Model Army A full-time, professional army formed by Oliver Cromwell during the Civil War

Parliament A collection of people representing all of England, who approve or refuse laws

Parliamentarians Those who are loyal to Parliament, often during a dispute with the king

Presbyterian A strong form of Protantism that took root in Scotland following the Reformation

Pride's Purge The expulsion of all but the most radical Members of Parliament in December 1648

Puritan A group of radical Protestants who wore plain clothing and tried to live without sin

Religious toleration A policy of allowing many different religions to exist within one state or country

Roundhead The nickname for Parliamentarian soldiers during the English Civil War

Royalists Those who are loyal to the king, often during a dispute with Parliament

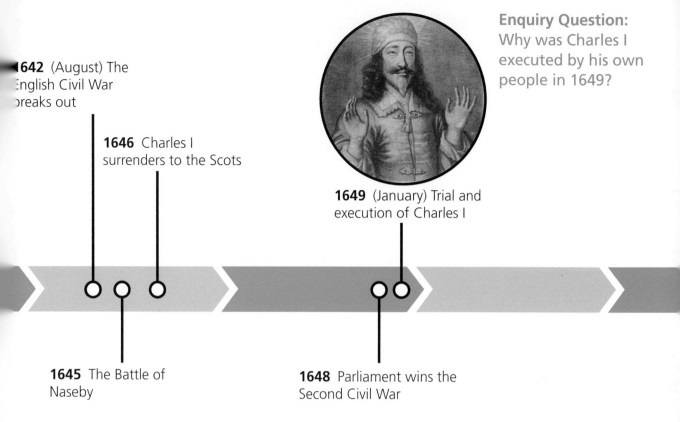

1642 (August) The English Civil War breaks out

1646 Charles I surrenders to the Scots

Enquiry Question: Why was Charles I executed by his own people in 1649?

1649 (January) Trial and execution of Charles I

1645 The Battle of Naseby

1648 Parliament wins the Second Civil War

Key vocabulary

Ship money A tax imposed on coastal towns to pay for their defence from naval attack

Star Chamber The English monarch's personal court, which did not have to give defendants a fair trial

State opening of Parliament The ceremony where England's monarch opens a session of Parliament

Stuarts The royal dynasty ruling England from 1603 to 1714

The eleven-years tyranny A period from 1629 during which Charles I ruled without calling Parliament

Touching for the king's evil The healing touch of a king for those who suffer from skin disease

Trainbands The City of London's volunteer militia, who fought for Parliament during the Civil War

Treason A crime against your own people, nation, or monarch

Key people

Charles I The second Stuart King of England, executed by Parliament following the Civil War

Guy Fawkes A leading member of the Gunpowder Plot, given responsibility to guard the explosives

Henrietta Maria Queen to Charles I, she was a Catholic and from France

James I First Stuart King of England, and son of Mary Queen of Scots

John Hampden Member of Parliament, who was tried and imprisoned for not paying ship money

John Pym Puritan Member of Parliament, and major opponent to Charles I before the Civil War

Prince Rupert Charles I's German nephew, appointed commander of the Royalist cavalry aged only 23

William Laud Archbishop of Canterbury who reintroduced some Catholic practices into church services

Unit 4: Commonwealth and Restoration
Cromwell's Commonwealth

The execution of Charles I astonished the people of England who, for the first time in their history, were not ruled by a monarch.

Instead, England was ruled by 140 Members of Parliament, nicknamed the '**Rump Parliament**', as only the most radical members had been allowed to remain following Pride's Purge. England was declared a '**Commonwealth**' on 16 May 1649, meaning it would be ruled in the common interest of the people. Three days later, the House of Lords was abolished. Many thought that they lived in a 'world turned upside-down'.

Ireland and Scotland

The Royalist cause still had strong support in Scotland and Ireland, and Parliament was afraid that England's neighbours could help Charles I's son (also named Charles) win back the crown. So, in 1649 they sent their best general, Oliver Cromwell, to defeat the Irish rebels.

Ireland was still a Catholic country. The only Protestants in Ireland were descended from Scottish and English settlers sent to Ireland by Elizabeth I and James I. These Protestant settlers had seized land from the native population, and mostly lived in the northern province of Ulster. Irish Catholics strongly disliked the Protestant settlers, and in 1641 there was an uprising against the Protestants known as the 'Portadown Massacre'.

Eight years later, Oliver Cromwell was out to seek revenge. Cromwell's treatment of the Irish Catholics was merciless. In the town of Drogheda, his troops killed 3500 civilians. Another 1500 civilians were killed in cold blood in Wexford. Worse still, Cromwell forced the Irish from their land, and those who resisted were sent to work as slaves on the Caribbean island of Barbados. Perhaps 200 000 Irish people died due to famine and war caused by Cromwell, and he is still remembered with hatred in many parts of Ireland today.

Cromwell saw things differently. He returned from his Irish campaign in 1650, and reported to Parliament "I am persuaded that this is a righteous judgement of God upon these barbarous wretches". A year later, Cromwell was sent to put down a rebellion in Scotland, where Royalists planned to invade England and put Charles I's son on the throne. Cromwell defeated the Scottish force twice, once at Dunbar in Scotland in 1650, and again at the Battle of Worcester in 1651. However, the young Charles managed to escape to France.

Lord Protector

Cromwell returned to England a war hero with 30 victories and no defeats on the battlefield. Cromwell believed in '**Godly Providence**', meaning that everything on earth happened due to God's will. It was easy for Cromwell to believe that God wanted him to win battles.

Contemporary print of Oliver Cromwell, accusing him of assuming the powers of a king

He also believed that it was God's wish for him to rule England. So, in 1653 Cromwell dismissed Parliament and made himself '**Lord Protector**'. Many urged him to become King Oliver, but Cromwell could not bring himself to do so. As Lord Protector, Cromwell still wore his simple black clothing and grey woollen socks.

In 1655, Cromwell appointed 11 Major-Generals to rule over the different regions of Britain, and used them to impose his Puritan beliefs. He banned theatre, dancing and pubs. On Sunday, it became illegal to go to buy or sell goods, or take part in sports such as bowling, horse racing and football. Cromwell even banned Christmas celebrations, as he saw them as an excuse for drunkenness and gluttony. For the first and only time in English history, the country was under a **military dictatorship**.

Cromwell's death

In 1658 Oliver Cromwell, the simple farmer who rose to be king in all but name, died. His son Richard became Lord Protector, but Richard Cromwell was a weak ruler without the stern authority of his father. He was nicknamed 'Tumbledown Dick', and after less than a year, he stepped down under pressure from the army. Oliver Cromwell's attempt to turn England into a Commonwealth was coming to an end.

Death mask of Oliver Cromwell

Oliver Cromwell

Oliver Cromwell was a member of the minor gentry from Huntingdon, near Cambridge. As a young man he appears to have suffered from severe depression, and he only recovered after converting to Puritanism during the late 1620s. Cromwell became intensely religious, and was elected to Parliament in 1628. He was descended from the sister of Thomas Cromwell, Henry VIII's chief minister who dissolved the monasteries. Clearly, Protestantism ran in the Cromwell family's blood.

Cromwell was a straightforward man, and not very good looking. Famously, he had warts on his face and a big nose. When his portrait was being painted, Cromwell is believed to have told the painter to depict him 'warts and all'.

Fact

Cromwell did have a genuine belief in the freedom of worship. For this reason in 1655, Jews were allowed back into England for the first time since Edward I banished them in 1290.

Check your understanding

1. Why did Parliament send their army to Ireland and Scotland after the end of the English Civil War?
2. What were the religious beliefs of the people in Ireland during this period?
3. Why is Oliver Cromwell still remembered with hatred in Ireland today?
4. What did Cromwell do to Parliament in 1653?
5. Once he became Lord Protector, what did Cromwell do to impose his Puritan beliefs?

The Restoration

It was clear England's Commonwealth experiment had failed under the rule of Tumbledown Dick. So, in 1660 the first elections in almost 20 years were held, and Parliament began negotiations with Charles I's son.

Coronation portrait of Charles II

The younger Charles was living in **exile** in Holland. Straightaway, he showed more willingness to compromise than his father. He issued a series of promises for what he would do as king, known as the **Declaration of Breda**. Charles promised religious toleration; rule alongside Parliament; and, most importantly, to take no revenge on those Parliamentarians who fought during the Civil War. After 20 years of bloody conflict, Charles II's Declaration offered England a chance to wipe the slate clean, and Parliament was happy to agree.

On 29 May 1660, the king was welcomed into London by ecstatic crowds. The writer John Evelyn recorded in his diary, "With a triumph of above 20 000 horse and foot, brandishing their swords and shouting with inexpressible joy; the ways strewed with flowers, the bells ringing, the streets hung with tapestry, fountains running wine… I stood in the Strand and beheld it, and blessed God".

The English monarchy had been restored, so this period has become known as the '**Restoration**'. Once king, the only revenge Charles II took was to execute the 59 **regicides** who signed his father's death warrant.

The Merry Monarch

Charles II did not care much about religion, and had an enormous thirst for enjoying life. He was nicknamed the '**Merry Monarch**'. Charles II wore magnificent clothes with a wig of long curly black hair, and particularly enjoyed drinking, gambling and dancing. He is known to have fathered at least 14 children with women who were not his wife. Once, when Charles II was introduced to an audience as 'Father of the English People', he joked that he had at least fathered a great number of them.

> ### Fact
>
> The regicides who had already died, including Oliver Cromwell, were exhumed, and had their corpses beheaded and their heads placed on spikes at Tyburn.

Painting of Charles II dancing with his sister Mary at a ball whilst in exile in Holland

Charles was witty and charming. However, he was notoriously untrustworthy and lacked principles. As his friend, the drunken poet Lord Rochester, wrote:

We have a pretty witty king,
Whose word no man relies on;
He never said a foolish thing,
Nor ever did a wise one.

As his reign continued, Charles II became less popular. His wild lifestyle and unsuccessful war against the Dutch caused high taxation. Charles II's financial situation became worse after London was hit by the plague in 1665, and the Great Fire in 1666. In 1667, England was humiliated when the Dutch navy sailed up the Medway and attacked the unsuspecting English navy, destroying half their ships and stealing the *Royal Charles* – England's greatest warship. However, nothing was quite so controversial as Charles II's approach to religion.

Religion

Charles II's French mother, Henrietta Maria, was a devout Catholic, and in 1668 his brother James, Duke of York secretly converted to Catholicism. In 1670, Charles II made a secret agreement with the French King Louis XIV promising to convert to Catholicism and to tolerate Catholics living in England. In return, Louis XIV paid Charles II 2 million *livres* every year.

Known as the **Treaty of Dover**, Charles kept his agreement a secret for many years, as there was a strong anti-Catholic feeling amongst the English people. After the English Civil War, enforcing conformity to the Church of England was seen as the only way of avoiding future conflict. In 1673, Parliament passed the **Test Act**, making allegiance to the Protestant Church of England compulsory for clergymen, teachers, and all those in government office. The king's own brother, James, Duke of York, had to step down as Lord High Admiral.

When Charles II died in 1685, he took the last rites of a Catholic. England was yet again faced with the same problem that dogged it for over a century. The dead monarch had no legitimate heir, and the next in line to the throne was a Catholic – his brother James.

Charles II's younger brother, James, Duke of York

Charles II's escape

The young Charles II was no stranger to adventure. After his defeat at the Battle of Worcester in 1651, he spent a night hiding in an oak tree. Disguised as a servant and calling himself Will Jackson, Charles travelled through England hunted by Parliament's troops and with a price of £1000 on his head. After six weeks he reached the coast, and sailed for France. Along the way ordinary people offered Charles II shelter, and this experience was said to have given him a rare ability to connect with his subjects.

Check your understanding

1. Why was Parliament happy to agree to Charles II returning to England as king in 1660?

2. How did Charles II deal with those who had fought for Parliament during the Civil War?

3. How would you describe the character of Charles II?

4. Why did Charles II keep his 1670 agreement with Louis XIV of France a secret?

5. Why was England faced with such a great problem after the death of Charles II in 1685?

Restoration England

After 10 years of Puritan rule, the English people welcomed the merry monarch Charles II. It was as if a grey cloud had been lifted from national life, allowing the sun to shine back in.

Alehouses, maypoles and Christmas celebrations all returned. Sunday sports were played, churches had music and choirs, local fairs were held, and theatres reopened. For the first time in English history, women were allowed to act on stage.

Fashions changed as well, as people once again wore colourful clothes, with lace, frills, silk and ribbons. Led by the king, a new fashion for wigs took off, and they became increasingly extravagant over the next 100 years. The Restoration is now remembered as a time of fun and frivolity.

Scientific revolution

In 1662, King Charles II gave a Royal Charter to a group of scientists, giving birth to the **Royal Society** of London for Improving Natural Knowledge. A great interest in science had developed in England during the 17th century. This was due in part to the Renaissance, but also to the Reformation, which encouraged people to move away from **superstition** and towards **rational thought**.

One member of the Royal Society was Robert Hooke, who built a compact microscope and was able to produce detailed drawings of insects, such as the flea. Earlier in the century, the English scientist William Harvey used a series of experiments to prove that blood circulates through the body, instead of being continually produced and consumed like fuel.

But the most important scientist of the period was, without doubt, Sir Isaac Newton. So the story goes, Newton was sitting under a tree when an apple fell on his head. This led him to wonder what forced the apple downwards, and the answer was gravity. Newton realised that all objects attract each other, depending on their mass and distance. This explains not only why an apple falls to the floor, but also why planets orbit the Sun. Newton explained the laws of gravity, and much more, in a book entitled *Principia Mathematica* and published in 1687. It is often described as the most important book in the history of science.

Newton was the first English scientist to be knighted, but he remained very modest. He compared himself to a boy playing with pebbles on the seashore, aware that "the great ocean of truth lay all undiscovered before me".

> **Fact**
>
> According to its original statute, women were not permitted to become fellows of the Royal Society, though an exception was made for Queen Victoria. This rule was only overturned in 1945.

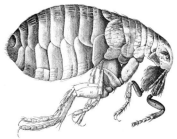

Robert Hooke's drawing of a flea, completed using his newly invented microscope in 1664

Sir Isaac Newton

The Great Plague

In 1665, the **plague** returned to England, and spread like wildfire through London where human, animal and food waste was often left rotting in the narrow, crowded streets. Hygiene was non-existent, especially for the poor, and 68 000 people died in a single year. Those who could afford it fled the city, and King Charles II took his royal court to Oxford.

Just like the attack of the plague during the Black Death of 1348, people had no idea why they were dying. The most popular theory was that plague spread through bad air, known as '**miasma**'. Plague doctors visited patients in an outfit designed to protect them from miasma. It consisted of a heavy waxed overcoat, glass goggles, a wooden cane for touching victims, and a 'beak' stuffed with scented substances such as dried flowers – designed to mask the bad air.

To prevent the spread of miasma, the mayor of London ordered that all dead bodies be collected and buried out of town, and the house in which they died be locked up and have a red cross painted on the door. Early each morning, body collectors roamed the streets of London ringing their bells and shouting, 'bring out your dead'. These measures had some positive effect in limiting the deaths, but it took a more destructive force to finally wipe out the plague: fire.

Illustration of men loading dead bodies into a cart during the plague of 1665.

Nell Gwyn

If one person summed up Restoration England, it was Charles II's mistress Nell Gwyn. An orange seller and actress from Covent Garden, she was a most unsuitable mistress for the king. However, Charles was entranced by her looks and wit. He took Nell Gwyn from the streets of Covent Garden to his royal palace, and had two children with her.

The English people loved 'pretty, witty Nelly'. On one occasion, Charles's coach was attacked by an angry mob, who accused Nell of being a 'Catholic whore'. She leaned out of the window and reassured them, 'I am the *Protestant* whore'. When Charles II died, he asked on his deathbed 'Let not poor Nelly starve'. She was provided with an annual pension of £1500 for the rest of her life.

Fact

During the Great Plague, 40 000 dogs and 200 000 cats were slaughtered as they were thought to be carrying the disease.

Check your understanding

1. How did life for normal English people change during the Restoration?
2. What other movements inspired England's scientific revolution during the 17th century?
3. What was Sir Isaac Newton's theory of gravity able to explain?
4. How was the response to the Great Plague different from the response to the Black Death in 1348?
5. Why was Nell Gwyn seen as an unsuitable mistress for the king?

Unit 4: Commonwealth and Restoration
The Great Fire of London

The summer of 1666 was long and hot. By the time September came, London's medieval houses, which were made out of wood and straw, were tinder-box dry.

The king's baker, Thomas Farynor, lived not far from London Bridge on Pudding Lane. On 2 September, he left his ovens on overnight cooking biscuits for the Royal Navy, and awoke to the smell of burning. Thomas escaped by jumping out of his window, but his bakery was soon engulfed in flames.

Thanks to a warm wind, the fire quickly spread to the riverside. Here, the warehouses of the London docks were full of flammable goods such as tallow, oil, timber and coal. Once these caught light, the fire was unstoppable. Soon, the flames were raging through London so quickly that people saw flying pigeons burned in the air.

Contemporary painting of the Great Fire, looking west across the Thames. St Paul's Cathedral can be seen engulfed in flames in the distance

Stopping the fire

It was left to the Mayor of London, Sir Thomas Bloodworth, to work out how to stop the fire. During the 17th century, there were no firemen or fire engines, and only the most basic water pumps and hoses. Teams of people lined up alongside the Thames passing leather buckets of water towards the flames. Even Charles II and his brother James took part in the fight. However, it made little difference and for three days, London was ablaze. The fire was so bright that at night an orange glow could be seen on the horizon 50 miles away in Oxford.

The only solution to the fire was to create '**firebreaks**'. To do this, rows of houses had to be pulled down with fire hooks or blown up with gunpowder, to create a barrier over which the fire could not pass. Many Londoners objected to having their houses or businesses, which had so far survived the flames, deliberately destroyed. However, the King overruled their objections, and the fire finally stopped on 7 September.

In all, the Great Fire claimed 13 200 houses, along with 87 churches, 44 merchant guildhalls, and all of the commercial buildings of the City of London. The medieval heart of England's capital was completely destroyed.

Rebuilding London

100 000 Londoners were left homeless by the fire and forced to live in tents outside the city. There was much speculation about how the fire began. Many rumours spread about Catholic plotters. A French watchmaker named Robert Hubert even admitted to starting the fire on the orders of the Pope, and was executed.

After the fire, Charles II set about the task of rebuilding London. To prevent another fire, it was firmly stated that buildings should only be constructed from brick or stone. The most talented architect of the day, Sir Christopher Wren, was tasked with designing a gleaming new London with wide streets, sewers and stone houses. At the centre of this new city was Wren's masterpiece: **St Paul's Cathedral**.

St Paul's Cathedral, London, England

Pepys' diary

Much can be learnt about life during the Restoration from a government official who worked in the Royal Navy named Samuel Pepys, who kept a wonderfully detailed diary from 1660 to 1669. It provides us with a unique insight into 17th century life.

Pepys was a sociable fellow, with connections at the royal court. He chatted to King Charles II on board the *Royal Charles*, the ship that brought him from Holland to England in 1660, and recorded: "…it made me weep to hear the stories he told of his difficulties he passed through".

Pepys was in London during the Great Fire, and took care to bury his most prized possession in his garden: a block of Parmesan cheese. On 3 September, he described seeing the crowds of people flee the city: "Lord! to see how the streets and the highways are crowded with people running and riding, and getting of carts at any rate to fetch away things. I am eased at my heart to have my treasure so well secured." The next day he wrote, "Only now and then walking into the garden, and saw how horridly the sky looks, all on a fire in the night." Pepys recorded how, as he walked towards central London during the fire, the road felt hot beneath his feet.

Samuel Pepys

Fact

Because the Great Fire took place in 1666, and the Great Plague attacked London the previous year, many believed that the four horsemen of the apocalypse were being sent to England as it was the 'year of the devil'.

Check your understanding

1. Why was London particularly vulnerable to fire at the end of the summer of 1666?
2. How did firebreaks stop the spread of the Great Fire?
3. What group of people were initially blamed for starting the Great Fire of London?
4. What rules did Christopher Wren have to follow when charged with rebuilding London after the fire?
5. Why is Samuel Pepys such an important guide for historians into life in 17th century England?

The Glorious Revolution

Despite having many children, Charles II died with no legitimate heir. This meant that his Catholic brother James II became king in 1685.

Many in England had feared this event. In 1679, a group in Parliament even tried to pass a bill excluding James II from the throne, but it was defeated in the House of Lords. A keen believer in the divine right of kings, James II dismissed Parliament the year that he was crowned.

Opponents to James II devised a new plan. The Duke of Monmouth was an **illegitimate** son of Charles II, and he was also a respected military commander and staunch Protestant. In 1685, Monmouth declared himself king and began a rebellion against James II in the West Country. James II's army easily defeated Monmouth's unimpressive force of 3000 men, and his response was savage.

James II, England's last Catholic monarch

Monmouth pleaded for forgiveness and promised to convert to Catholicism, but he was executed. Of his supporters, 850 were sent to the West Indies to work as slaves, and 480 were executed. Their severed heads were pickled in jars of vinegar and sent around England, as a warning to those who would still consider rebelling against their new king.

James II's reign

James II then began suspending the Test Acts, allowing Catholics back into public office. Protestant clergymen who criticised James II were tried for treason. James and his second wife, an Italian Catholic called Mary of Modena, had been married for 15 years and were childless. But then in June 1688, Mary gave birth to a son, also called James. This startling news all but guaranteed a Catholic future for the English throne.

The Duke of Monmouth

England's leading Protestants knew they had to act. Previously, James II had been married to an Englishwoman, Anne Hyde. With her, he had had two daughters, and the eldest – Mary – was third in line to the throne. She was married to the Dutch prince William of Orange, who also happened to be a grandson of Charles I, and Mary's first cousin. William and Mary were both staunch Protestants. On 30 June 1688, a group of seven leading English politicians wrote to William of Orange imploring him to invade England, and rid them of their Catholic king.

The Glorious Revolution

In the autumn of 1688, William of Orange began assembling an enormous invasion force of 463 ships and 40 000 troops in Holland. On 5 November they landed off the coast of Devon.

James II was outraged: his own daughter and son-in-law had invaded England to seize his crown. But James doubted whether he could rely on the support of the English people, so he decided not to fight. Increasingly

Fact

Many Protestants refused to believe that James II's son with Mary of Modena was real. A rumour spread that he was a miller's son, smuggled into the royal bed in a long-handled warming pan.

distraught, James II suffered a mental breakdown, and on 11 December he fled the Palace of Whitehall for exile in France. As he sailed from his palace, he threw the **Great Seal** of England into the Thames. Six weeks later, on 13 February 1689, William and Mary were crowned joint King and Queen of England.

Some historians claim it was an invasion, others claim it was a liberation, but all agree the events of 1688 changed England forever. This event later became known as the '**Glorious Revolution**'. It was a 'Revolution' because the people of England had ejected a Catholic absolutist as king, and replaced him with a Protestant king who was willing to rule with Parliament. It was 'Glorious' because not a single drop of blood was shed in the process. To secure the support of Parliament, William and Mary signed an agreement in 1689 called the Bill of Rights. This was a landmark document in securing legal and political rights for the people of England. Like Magna Carta before it, the Bill of Rights constrained the power of the English monarch.

Contemporary painting of William III's invasion force leaving Holland for England on 19th October, 1688

James II did not give up his claim to the English throne, and launched a rebellion from Ireland. He was defeated at the Battle of the Boyne in 1690, and went into exile with his wife and son in France, and then Rome. After 40 years of absolutism, civil war, regicide, dictatorship, restoration and invasion, Parliament finally had their rights established in law. An absolute monarch would never again rule England.

The Bill of Rights

Some clauses of the Bill of Rights included:

- No Catholic could sit on the English throne

- Members of Parliament should have freedom of speech within Parliament (a principle known as Parliamentary prerogative)

- No taxes could be imposed on the people without the agreement of Parliament

- The king should not have a standing army during peacetime without the agreement of Parliament

- The king could not create or suspend laws without the agreement of Parliament

Check your understanding

1. Once made king, how did James II try to rule as an 'absolute monarch'?
2. Who were William and Mary, and what was their claim to the throne?
3. Why is William and Mary's invasion known as the Glorious Revolution?
4. How did the Bill of Rights ensure the power of Parliament was established in law?
5. What became of James II following the Glorious Revolution?

Unit 4: Commonwealth and Restoration
Knowledge organiser

1649 (May) England is declared a Commonwealth

1653 Oliver Cromwell becomes 'Lord Protector'

1660 Charles II is crowned King of England, beginning the Restoration

1651 The future Charles II is defeated at the Battle of Worcester

1658 Death of Oliver Cromwell

Key vocabulary

Commonwealth The period when England ceased to be a monarchy, and was at first ruled by Parliament

Declaration of Breda A series of promises made by Charles II prior to his restoration as king

Exile Being forced to live outside your native country, typically for political reasons

Firebreak A manmade gap in combustible material used to prevent the further spread of fire

Glorious Revolution The peaceful rejection of James II as king, and replacement by William and Mary

Godly Providence A belief that events are governed by the direct intervention of God in the world

Great Seal A seal used to show the monarch's approval of important state documents

Illegitimate Not recognised as lawful, once used to describe someone born of unmarried parents

Lord Protector The title given to Oliver Cromwell as head of the English state and the Church of England

Merry Monarch Nickname given to Charles II due to his wit, lack of seriousness, and fun-loving lifestyle

Miasma The theory that disease is caused by the spreading smell of a poisonous cloud of 'bad air'

Military dictatorship A form of government where the military hold sole power over the state

Plague The most common variant is Bubonic plague, named after the swellings on victims' bodies

Rational thought The idea that reasoning, not superstition, should be the source of human knowledge

Regicide The deliberate killing of a monarch, or the person responsible for doing so

Restoration The return of the monarchy to England with Charles II's coronation in 1660

Royal Society A group founded in 1660 for the advancement of scientific knowledge

Rump Parliament The remaining members of the Parliament after it was purged before Charles I's trial

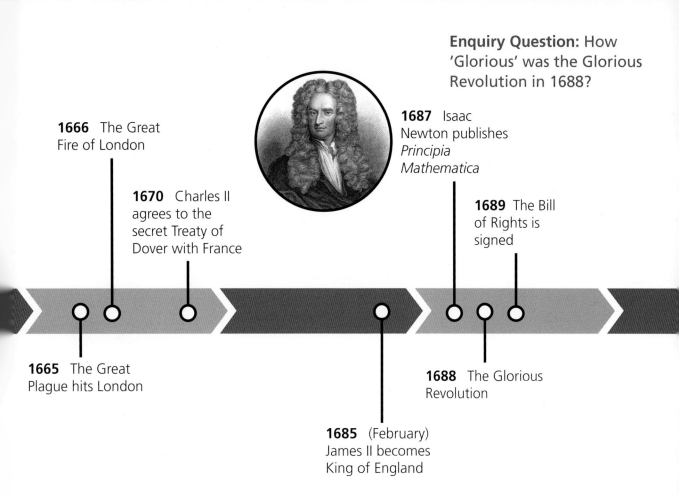

1666 The Great Fire of London

1670 Charles II agrees to the secret Treaty of Dover with France

1687 Isaac Newton publishes *Principia Mathematica*

1689 The Bill of Rights is signed

1665 The Great Plague hits London

1688 The Glorious Revolution

1685 (February) James II becomes King of England

Key people

Charles II The King of England following the Restoration

Duke of Monmouth Illegitimate son of Charles II who led a rebellion against James II and was executed

James II The brother of Charles II, who was forced to abdicate after three years of absolutist rule

Nell Gwyn Charles II's mistress rose from being an actress to being a member of the royal court

Oliver Cromwell A Parliamentary cavalry general, who became Lord Protector of England

Samuel Pepys Official in the Royal Navy during the reign of Charles II, who kept a famous diary

Sir Christopher Wren Architect who rebuilt St Paul's Cathedral following the Great Fire of London

Sir Isaac Newton A great scientist, often said to be the founder of modern physics

William and Mary Joint monarchs from 1688: one a Dutch prince, the other a daughter of James II

Key vocabulary

Scientific Revolution The emergence of modern scientific methods during the 17th and 18th centuries

St Paul's Cathedral Historic London Cathedral, destroyed during and rebuilt after the Great Fire

Superstition The belief in supernatural powers, in place of rational explanation

Test Act A law requiring all those who held public office to be Protestants

The Bill of Rights A document establishing Parliament's rights and limitations to the Monarch's power

Treaty of Dover A secret treaty in which Charles II promised Louis XIV he would convert to Catholicism

Creation of Great Britain

William and Mary, who became joint king and queen following the Glorious Revolution, were succeeded by Mary's sister Anne in 1702. Queen Anne was England's last Stuart monarch.

Anne's life was cursed with bad luck. She suffered from a horrible illness called **gout**, and not one of her 18 children survived long enough to succeed her. Anne had seven miscarriages, six stillbirths, and five children who died young. Despite all of these troubles, she was a wise and important queen, and it was during her reign that the nation of **Great Britain** was created.

The creation of Great Britain

Parliament was very worried about Queen Anne's lack of children. Her Catholic half-brother James Stuart, son of James II, had been brought up in France and believed that he should be king of England. He had the support of the powerful kings of France and Spain.

Statue of Queen Anne, beside St Paul's Cathedral, London, England

To avoid another civil war, the English Parliament had passed the **Act of Settlement** in 1701, declaring that when Anne died, the crown would pass to her nearest Protestant relative. Most people in England were happy with the settlement, but the Scottish people were not. Since 1603 the same monarch had ruled Scotland and England, but they had remained two separate countries, with two separate parliaments.

The Scots were furious that they were not consulted about who would succeed Queen Anne. Many in Scotland liked the idea of being ruled by James Stuart. The Stuart family was originally from Scotland, and a number of powerful Scottish families were still Catholics. So, in 1703 the Scottish Parliament declared that when Queen Anne died, they would choose their own monarch. This would have broken the 100-year union between the English and Scottish crowns.

The English were very worried about this development. They proposed to Scotland that their two countries should become one, sharing one monarch, with one Parliament based in Westminster. At first the Scots disliked this idea: the English writer Daniel Defoe travelled to Scotland and reported: "for every Scot in favour there is 99 against".

However, the Scottish people had recently invested £500 000 (half the nation's available capital) in an adventurous plan to establish a Scottish colony in Central America, known as the **Darien Scheme**. It was a terrible failure, and very nearly bankrupted the country. Therefore, the English

> **Fact**
>
> Anne formed intensely emotional bonds with her female courtiers. For most of her reign her favourite courtier was Sarah Churchill, the Duchess of Marlborough. When Anne's affections moved on to Sarah's cousin, Abigail, Sarah spread rumours that Queen Anne and Abigail were in a sexual relationship.

Parliament was able to win round the Scottish leaders with some very generous bribes. The Scottish Parliament agreed to vote itself into non-existence. On 1 May 1707, the **Act of Union** was passed. The Scottish poet Robert Burns later wrote of the Act, "We're bought and sold for English gold, such a parcel of rogues in a nation!"

The first article of the Act of Union declared "That the two Kingdoms of England and Scotland shall upon the first day of May… be united into one Kingdom by the name of Great Britain." The Act also described the flag that this new country would use, combining the diagonal white cross of St Andrew, and the red cross of St George. This new national flag was nicknamed the '**Union Jack**'.

The Hanoverian succession

Queen Anne had been ill for many years, and died in 1714. Her doctor wrote, "I believe sleep was never more welcome to a weary traveller than death was to her". So, Parliament set about searching Europe for Anne's closest surviving Protestant relative to be her successor. The answer was found in the shape of Georg Ludwig, the 54-year-old ruler of a small German state called Hanover. He just happened to be the great-grandson of James I.

Georg Ludwig arrived in London on 18 September with a procession of 260 horse-drawn carriages, and was crowned George I of Great Britain a month later. Britain now had a new royal family, known as the **Hanoverians**.

For many people, it was a strange sight. There were 57 Catholic descendents of the Stuarts across Europe with a better claim to the English throne than George I. Before being plucked from obscurity to become King, George I had only visited England once in his life. He spoke no English and took very little interest in the country, preferring to spend his time playing cards, visiting Germany, and entertaining his two mistresses. They were nicknamed the elephant and the maypole because one was very fat, and the other was very thin.

> ### Fact
>
> George I was famous for his temper. While he was Elector of Hanover, he had found out his wife was unfaithful, so he locked her in a tower for the rest of her life.

Painting of George I, who went from ruling a small German state to becoming King of Great Britain in 1714

> ### Check your understanding
>
> **1.** Why were many people in Scotland opposed to the Act of Settlement?
> **2.** Why did the English Parliament propose in 1703 that England and Scotland become one country?
> **3.** How did the English Parliament manage to win round the Scots into supporting the Act of Union?
> **4.** Why did George I become king in 1714 when 57 people across Europe had a better claim to the throne?
> **5.** Where had George I ruled before he was crowned King of Great Britain?

Parliamentary government

Although George I was king, he knew almost nothing about how to rule Britain. For this reason he relied on his ministers, normally Members of Parliament, to make decisions on his behalf.

After an unhappy century of absolutist monarchs causing disagreements and wars, this new situation suited Parliament very nicely. From now on, the monarch reigned but ministers ruled.

The first Prime Minister

Robert Walpole was a wealthy farmer from Norfolk and a Member of Parliament. He weighed 20 stone, loved drinking and eating, and had ambitions to become the most powerful politician in Britain. Walpole's political career took off after an economic crash called **the South Sea Bubble** (see box). Walpole was made Paymaster General and successfully restored Britain's economy, becoming George I's favourite **minister** as a result.

Britain's first Prime Minister, Sir Robert Walpole

Walpole was not an honest man. He would bribe other politicians to get his way. As a young man he even spent six months imprisoned in the Tower of London for corruption! One of his favourite sayings was that "all men have their price". However, Walpole was a popular figure and good at his job.

In 1721, Walpole was given three of the key jobs in British politics: First Lord of the Treasury, Chancellor of the Exchequer and Leader of the **House of Commons**. This made him the most important minister in the King's Government, so people would refer to him as the **'prime' minister**. The king gave him a house in London

10 Downing Street, London, England

to live in, and selected number 10 on a new development near Parliament called 'Downing Street'. Walpole recommended that the house should forever remain the property of whoever held his position. To this day the Prime Minister of Great Britain lives at number **10 Downing Street**.

Parliamentary government

In 1727 King George I died, and his son George II became king. George II spoke a bit more English, but with a heavy German accent. He thought Walpole had become too powerful as Prime Minister, and tried to replace him. However, Walpole promised George II that, if he was kept as Prime Minister, he would increase the king's allowance. Since the Glorious Revolution, Parliament controlled the monarch's annual allowance – something known as the 'power of the purse'. So, George II decided to let Walpole keep his job.

> **Fact**
>
> In 1755 George II visited Hanover and considered not returning to Britain because he was so angry at the growing power of Parliament. He complained, "Ministers are the kings in this country, I am nothing there."

As Prime Minister, Walpole had two ambitions: to stay out of any foreign wars, and to keep taxes low. He succeeded, and Britain grew wealthy as her foreign trade flourished. Walpole once boasted to Queen Caroline, the wife of George II, "Madam, there are 50 000 men slain this year in Europe, and not one Englishman".

During the 20 years that Walpole was in power, he established '**parliamentary government**' in Great Britain. In theory the king could choose his government ministers, but in reality he could only choose those with the support of the most powerful party in Parliament. Parliament was, as it still is today, split into two 'Houses': the Commons and the Lords. Seats in the House of Commons went to Members of Parliament elected by the British public, though only a small

Painting of the Prime Minister addressing the House of Commons, from the end of the 18th century

minority of wealthy men had the vote. Most seats in the **House of Lords** passed down through generations of noble families along with hereditary titles, which were – in order of importance – Duke, Marquess, Earl, Viscount and Baron.

By this time, two rival political parties had developed in Parliament, each with different ideas about how England should be governed. One party wanted to limit the power of the king and allow greater tolerance for religious groups. They were nicknamed '**Whigs**' – an old Scottish insult for Presbyterian rebels. The other group wanted to protect the power of the king and the Church of England. They were nicknamed '**Tories**' – an old Irish word for a Catholic outlaw.

The South Sea Bubble

The South Sea Bubble was one of the greatest economic disasters in British history. Exclusive rights to trade with Spanish colonies in South America were granted to the South Sea Company, and company **shares** became highly sought after. Over the spring of 1720, its share price increased by ten times, but then the bubble burst and the share price came crashing down.

Thousands of normal citizens who had invested in the company were made bankrupt overnight, company directors fled the country, and a spate of suicides took place. One government minister, Lord Stanhope, even died of a stroke during an angry debate in Parliament.

Check your understanding:
1. How did Robert Walpole become George I's favourite minister?
2. How was the role of Prime Minster established during Walpole's time in power?
3. How did the system of parliamentary government, established by Walpole, function?
4. Why did George II consider not returning from Hanover when he visited in 1755?
5. What caused the South Sea Bubble to take place?

Jacobite uprisings

Most people in Britain were by now happy with their new German kings, but a small group retained a passionate belief that the Stuart royal family should still be governing Britain.

These people called themselves '**Jacobites**', a name taken from the Latin word for 'James'. They formed secret societies across England and Scotland, and plotted to overthrow the Hanoverian kings. In 1715, a small Jacobite rebellion failed to place James II's son, James Stuart, on the throne. But they kept on plotting – waiting for the right moment to act.

Bonnie Prince Charlie

By 1745 the British army was busy fighting the French in Europe, so the Jacobites spotted a chance. Support for the Stuart claim to the throne was strongest in the mountains and moors of the Scottish **Highlands**. Ancient '**clans**' ruled this part of Scotland, and each clan was led by a 'chief'. The clansmen were mostly poor Catholic farmers, but they were also fierce warriors who believed the 1707 Act of Union had robbed Scotland of its independence.

The Jacobites found a new hope in James Stuart's eldest son, Charles Edward Stuart, who was a charismatic and brave soldier. He was also very good looking, so his Highland supporters named him 'Bonnie Prince Charlie' – 'Bonnie' meaning good-looking in Scotland. Prince Charlie landed in Scotland in July 1745, and the Highland clans rushed to welcome him. They raised enough men to take Edinburgh, the capital city of Scotland, and routed the small British army in Scotland at the Battle of Prestonpans.

Painting of Bonnie Prince Charlie with two clan chiefs, completed in 1892

The Highlanders wore Scottish **tartan** and caps with white cockades, and armed themselves with traditional Scottish swords called **claymores**. With these soldiers, Prince Charlie won a series of victories in Scotland, and by November his 6000 men were marching south towards London. With most of his army fighting in France, King George II was terrified. He even loaded a boat on the Thames with treasure so that he could make an easy escape if Prince Charlie's army arrived in London.

Prince Charlie expected that England's Jacobites, who for years had held underground meetings and identified each other through secret symbols, would rush to his support when he invaded England. When the moment came, however, most were not brave enough to risk their lives. Prince Charlie marched as far south as Derby, but his soldiers grew disheartened about the lack of support from the English people. On 5 December 1745, the Jacobite army began its retreat back to the Scottish Highlands.

The Battle of Culloden

By now, George II had raised an army led by his son the Duke of Cumberland and put a price of £30 000 on Prince Charlie's head.

Cumberland's red-coated soldiers shadowed the retreating Jacobites to the Highlands of Scotland, where they met for a final battle at Culloden Moor in April 1746. Cumberland defeated the Jacobite army in less than an hour, tearing them apart with his cannons and cavalry.

Bonnie Prince Charlie escaped from the battlefield, and for weeks he hid in the moors of Scotland. According to legend, he was found by a young woman named Flora MacDonald who planned his escape. MacDonald disguised Prince Charlie as her Irish maid, and he took a boat to the Isle of Skye, and from there he escaped to France.

Prince Charlie lived the rest of his life in exile in Italy. The Stuart cause was dead, and the Hanoverians were safely established as Britain's royal family. Culloden remains the last ever battle to be fought on British soil.

> **Fact**
>
> Prince Charlie died in Rome on 31 January 1788, the anniversary of his great-great-grandfather Charles I's execution in 1649.

Contemporary painting of the Battle of Culloden

Suppression of the Highlands

The British Government wanted to make sure that no Jacobite rising could ever happen again. Cumberland hunted down and killed all of the remaining Jacobite soldiers with such savagery that he became known as 'the Butcher'. The British Government did not stop there. They made it illegal for Highlanders to wear their traditional dress of tartan and kilts, or to own weapons. The right of the chiefs to rule their own clans was abolished, and many Highland farmers were forced to move to the Scottish lowlands, or emigrate to America.

A large barracks named **Fort George** was built outside Inverness so that the British army could keep a watchful eye on their troublesome fellow countrymen north of the border. From now on, the Scottish Highlands were firmly under the control of the British Government.

Memorial to the Jacobites, at Glenfinnan, Highlands, Scotland

---

Check your understanding:

1. Why did Jacobites oppose the Hanoverian kings?
2. Why did many of Scotland's highland clans support Bonnie Prince Charlie?
3. Why did Bonnie Prince Charlie's army retreat back to Scotland in December 1745?
4. What happened at the Battle of Culloden?
5. How did the British government ensure that no Jacobite rising could ever happen again in Scotland?

Georgian aristocracy

Parliamentary government in Georgian Britain may have weakened the power of the monarch, but power did not move to the people.

Instead, power became increasingly concentrated in the hands of Britain's nobility, leading many historians to call the 18th century the 'Age of **Aristocracy**'. There were 173 **peers** in the House of Lords in 1700, and the great majority of government ministers came from this closed circle of titled landowners. England's first 10 Prime Ministers included three dukes, one marquess, two earls, and two who became earls during their lifetime.

Powerful families such as the Temples dominated English politics: Earl Temple and all four of his brothers served as members of Parliament, with one – George Grenville – becoming Prime Minister. Meanwhile, their sister Hester married William Pitt, who later became Prime Minister and the Earl of Chatham, and whose son, Pitt the Younger, also served as Prime Minister.

When a peer had no sons to inherit his title, it would become extinct, so the king regularly had to create new peerages. However, breaking into this class from a humble background was almost impossible: of the 229 peerages created between 1700 and 1800, only 23 had no previous connection with the aristocracy. Though they sat in the House of Lords, the aristocracy still held influence over elections to the House of Commons. MPs in the Commons were often related by birth or marriage to the aristocracy, and in 1715, 224 of the 558 members of the House of Commons were the sons of MPs.

The Georgian aristocracy grew increasingly wealthy during this period, often acquiring more land from the gentry, whose wealth was in decline. Aristocratic stately homes, such as Castle Howard and Blenheim Palace, remain some of the most extravagant buildings in Britain. **Wentworth Woodhouse** in Yorkshire, home to the 2nd Marquess of Rockingham (who became Prime Minister in 1765), is Britain's largest stately home, with over 300 rooms.

Painting of Mr and Mrs Andrews, a wealthy couple from the landed gentry, completed in 1750

Wentworth Woodhouse in Yorkshire, England

Fact

A powerful Whig politician, Charles James Fox, inherited one of the largest fortunes in Georgian England, but he loved to gamble. Fox went bankrupt twice, had his furniture confiscated by bailiffs, and by the time of his death had gambled away £200 000 – perhaps £18 million in today's money.

Leisure and entertainment

The Georgian aristocracy and gentry certainly knew how to enjoy themselves. Horse racing, card games, hunting, theatre, the opera and – most notably – gambling were all popular amongst the Georgian elite. They drank and gambled at exclusive London clubs such as Brooks' and White's, and visited fashionable holiday towns such as Brighton and Bath, which are still famous for their fine Georgian architecture.

Scene from *Marriage à la mode*, a series of paintings by William Hogarth satirising aristocratic life

For half of the year, from January to June, Parliament was in session, so the aristocracy decamped from their country estates to their smart London townhouses. Known as the '**season**', this period was accompanied by a whirl of glamorous parties and events. A collection of fields to the west of London where the May Fair took place each year, had recently been developed by its owner Sir Thomas Grosvenor into townhouses. This new development became known as Mayfair, and at its centre lay Grosvenor Square, the most fashionable address in London.

Having the right tastes in fashion and art was very important to the Georgian aristocracy, and they often acted as patrons to young writers and artists. For the sons of Britain's aristocracy, the best way to finish their education was to undertake a '**Grand Tour**' of Europe. Lasting around two years, young aristocratic men on a Grand Tour learned about the culture and history of Europe – in particular Italy.

While travelling, these young aristocrats bought artefacts from Ancient Rome, fashionable European clothes, and paintings by celebrated artists, such as the Venetian painter Canaletto. However, many young aristocrats set free in Europe took a different path, spending their money on drinking, gambling and womanising instead.

Samuel Johnson

The son of a poor bookseller from Lichfield, Samuel Johnson worked his way to the University of Oxford and onwards to becoming one of the greatest writers in the English language. He was famously ugly, and had lots of nervous tics. However, because he was so witty and intelligent, his company was highly sought after by the Georgian aristocracy. Following his death, Johnson left his estate to Francis Barber, his servant and a Black Jamaican who had formerly been enslaved. Barber's descendants still farm near Lichfield today.

After 10 years of work, Johnson published one of the first English language dictionaries in 1755. It contained the definitions for 40 000 words. These included some amusing entries. Johnson defined 'dull' as "Not exhilarating; not delightful; as, to make dictionaries is dull work".

Check your understanding

1. How many aristocratic peers were there in England at the beginning of the 18th century?

2. How did the aristocracy still have power over the House of Commons?

3. Why did the aristocracy spend half of the year in London, and half of the year in their stately homes?

4. What would young aristocrats do while they undertook the Grand Tour?

5. What achievement is Samuel Johnson best remembered for?

Poverty, violence and crime

While the power and wealth of Georgian Britain flowed to the aristocracy, many in Britain's towns and cities lived lives of poverty, violence and crime.

Some of the worst poverty was to be found in London, where people moved to find work, but sudden joblessness could make them destitute. The poorest families lived in single, unfurnished rooms, with no running water or sanitation.

For those who could not afford a room, vagrancy was the only alternative. It was not uncommon to find dead bodies on the streets of major cities, particularly on cold winter mornings. For women who fell into poverty, there was often no alternative but to work in the sex trade, something Georgian men exploited openly. Between 1757 and 1795, an annual guide to London's female sex workers was published, entitled *Harris's List of Covent Garden Ladies*.

William Hogarth's print *Gin Lane*, showing the social consequences of gin addiction amongst the Georgian poor

Many of the poor drowned their sorrows with a newly popular drink called gin. Cheap and strong, it was said that in 1730s London there was a shop selling gin for every 11 people. George II's Vice-Chamberlain observed, "the whole town of London swarmed with drunken people from morning till night". Gin was blamed for a host of social problems, from violence and robberies to murders, irreligion and child mortality. This can be seen in the vivid print *Gin Lane*, created by William Hogarth in 1751 (see box).

Whenever Parliament tried to control the trade of gin with licensing acts, the people of London would riot. In 1736, Parliament introduced an annual £50 licence which shopkeepers had to buy in order to sell gin. In response, angry crowds spread through London chanting "No gin, no king!" The 1751 Gin Act succeeded in placing a tax on the drink, and began a decline in gin's popularity.

Law and order

Georgian Britain could be a strikingly violent place. The right to bear arms was enshrined in the 1689 Bill of Rights, so that the Protestant population could arm themselves against the Catholic threat. Members of the aristocracy commonly carried swords, and pistols were easy to purchase. As the century went on, these weapons were increasingly used for violent crime.

There was no organised police force in Georgian Britain. While smaller towns and villages were able to govern themselves, in the growing towns and cities violent crime became a severe problem. Criminals would break

Fact

Even dead bodies would be stolen in Georgian England. 'Body snatchers' robbed newly dug graves, and sold the corpses to trainee doctors and anatomists who used them for dissections.

into houses, rob passers-by on the streets, and steal cargo from ships. Crime waves often followed the end of foreign wars, when industry would slump due to the army no longer needing supplies, and soldiers would return home unable to find jobs.

For criminals facing trial, Georgian prisons were frequently likened to hell on earth. Many prisons were run as private, profit-making organisations, so prisoners were kept in horrific conditions to keep costs low. Human waste lined the floors of overcrowded and windowless cells, which were freezing cold in the winter and unbearably hot in the summer. Newgate was the most notorious of all London's prisons. During the 18th century, Newgate suffered repeated outbreaks of typhus, a fatal disease spread by lice. Prisoners would often escape by breaking through the floor of their cells and exiting through the sewer.

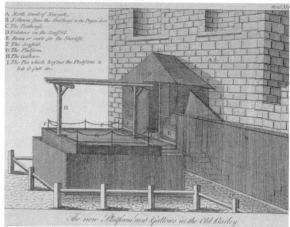

Platform and gallows at Newgate Prison, Old Bailey, City of London, 1783

Highwaymen

The 18th century saw an increase in **highwaymen**: armed robbers on horseback who attacked people travelling in **stagecoaches** along dark, empty roads. The use of cheques only became common during the second half of the century, so people often had to carry large sums of money in person. Travellers came to dread the sound of galloping hooves and pistol shots, followed by the infamous cry "Stand and Deliver! Your money or your life!"

The most well-known highwayman was Dick Turpin. Today he is remembered as a dashing hero, but in reality he was a convicted murderer who terrorised the roads of Essex until he was hanged at York in 1739.

Grave and headstone of Dick Turpin

William Hogarth

Perhaps the greatest artist of Georgian Britain was William Hogarth. His father was an impoverished Latin teacher, and Hogarth spent his childhood drawing caricatures of London street life. He came to specialise in **satirical** cartoons, often criticising the moral failings of Georgian society, such as its addiction to gin.

Hogarth's works liked to tell a story. His series of paintings known as *A Rake's Progress* follows the son of a wealthy merchant who wastes all of his money on fine clothes, women and gambling, before becoming bankrupt and being sent to a mental asylum.

Check your understanding

1. In cities such as London, what sort of conditions did the poorest in society have to live in?
2. What happened when Parliament tried to control the sale of gin during the 18th century?
3. Why was crime particularly serious during the Georgian period following the end of foreign wars?
4. Why did 18th century highwaymen target people who were travelling?
5. What were conditions like in 18th century prisons?

Unit 5: Georgian Britain
Knowledge organiser

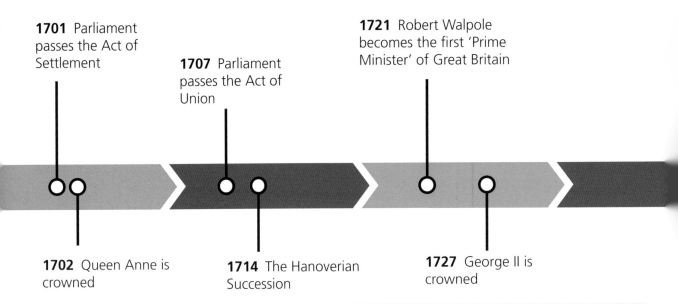

1701 Parliament passes the Act of Settlement

1707 Parliament passes the Act of Union

1721 Robert Walpole becomes the first 'Prime Minister' of Great Britain

1702 Queen Anne is crowned

1714 The Hanoverian Succession

1727 George II is crowned

Key vocabulary

10 Downing Street Traditional home of the English Prime Minister since the reign of George I

Act of Settlement A law passed in 1701 ensuring that a Protestant would succeed Queen Anne

Act of Union A law which united England and Scotland in 1707, and created Great Britain

Aristocracy The government of a country by an elite class, often with hereditary titles

Clan Ancient family from the Highlands of Scotland

Claymore A traditional Scottish sword

Darien Scheme A failed attempt by the Scottish government to establish a Caribbean trading colony

Fort George A large British barracks built in the Scottish Highlands following Jacobite defeat

Gout An illness caused by heavy eating or drinking, which causes joints to become swollen

Grand Tour Journey taken by upper class young men to experience the art and culture of Europe

Great Britain A name given to the island comprising England, Wales and Scotland

Hanoverians A royal dynasty that ruled England from 1714 until 1837

Highlands A sparsely populated area of northern Scotland known for its mountainous landscape

Highwaymen Armed robbers on horseback who attacked people travelling in stagecoaches

House of Commons The 'lower house' in Parliament, where seats go to MPs elected by the people

House of Lords The 'upper house' in Parliament, where seats are inherited by members of the peerage

Jacobite Supporters of the Stuart claim to the throne, following the exile of James II

Minister A politician with a central role within the nation's government

Parliamentary government A political system where ministers must be chosen from the most powerful party in Parliament

Peer A member of the House of Lords who, for most of English history, were from the nobility

Prime Minister The most senior post in the British government, first held by Sir Robert Walpole

Satirical Using humour to criticise human failings, often in the context of politics

Season A six-month period when Parliament was in session and the aristocracy came to London

Share A portion of a company that can be bought, bringing with it a portion of the profits

1739 The highwayman Dick Turpin is hanged in York

1746 The Battle of Culloden

1751 Parliament passes the Gin Act

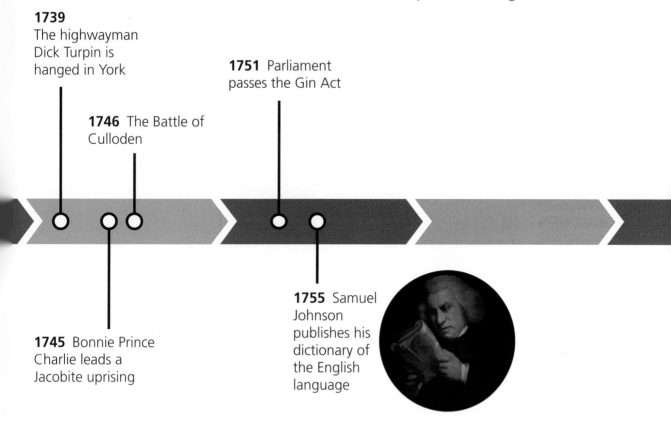

1745 Bonnie Prince Charlie leads a Jacobite uprising

1755 Samuel Johnson publishes his dictionary of the English language

Key people

Bonnie Prince Charlie The last Stuart claimant to Britain's throne, and leader of a failed rebellion in 1745

Dick Turpin Legendary 18th century highwayman from Essex

Duke of Cumberland Son of George II, nicknamed 'the Butcher' for his suppression of the Highlands

George I The first Hanoverian King of England, previously a minor German prince

Queen Anne The last Stuart monarch, who created the union between England and Scotland

Robert Walpole A major Georgian statesman, generally seen as Britain's first Prime Minister

Samuel Johnson Famous Georgian writer, author of one of the first dictionaries of the English language

William Hogarth English satirical artist, his best-known works are *Gin Lane* and *A Rake's Progress*

Key vocabulary

Stagecoach A horse-drawn carriage used for long distance travel

Suppression A dominant political power limiting the freedom and activity of a group of people

Tartan Traditional patterned cloth of Scotland, often used to make kilts

The South Sea Bubble An economic disaster caused by the sudden drop in share price of a colonial trading company

Tories A political party which originally formed to protect the power of the king

Union Jack Nickname for the national flag of Great Britain

Whigs A political party which originally formed to limit the power of the king

Unit 6: Renaissance Europe
The Renaissance

Compared with the scholars of the Islamic world, and the scientific advances of the Song dynasty in China, Europe was not at the forefront of advancing human knowledge during the medieval period.

This situation began to change during the 15th century. Starting in Italy, Europeans took a new interest in the cultural achievements of their **classical** forebears – the Ancient Greeks and Romans. While much classical writing had been forgotten within medieval Europe, it was kept alive by the scholars of the Islamic world and the Byzantine Empire. Due to the increased contact with the Islamic world during the Crusades, and the fall of Constantinople in 1453 (see box), classical drama, poetry, science, mythology, philosophy and political thought began to find its way back into Europe.

The School of Athens, painted by Raphael in 1509, depicts the greatest thinkers of the classical world

At the same time, scholars were increasingly broadening their concerns away from religious learning and towards the study of humankind. They also could now study classical texts in their original forms, rather than in translations that might distort the meaning. A new term emerged to describe these developments: **humanism**. This change was helped by the growth of universities. The first European university was founded in the Italian city of Bologna in 1088, and universities in Oxford, Paris and Salamanca soon followed. By 1500, there were 62 universities in Europe where students could study subjects such as law, philosophy, medicine and mathematics.

The combination of new learning in the universities with the rediscovery of classical ideas in the 15th century led to a period of extraordinary artistic and cultural flourishing in Europe. This was known as 'the **Renaissance**', meaning 'rebirth' in French.

Italian city states

While feudal monarchs ruled most of medieval Europe, a small number of Italian cities were different. These were independent **city states**, which governed themselves and their surrounding area, and were able to develop a distinctive character of their own. As urban centres, the Italian city states were home to Europe's most successful trade guilds, craftsmen, merchants and bankers – making them extremely wealthy. The city states' most powerful figures demonstrated their importance by becoming **patrons** of the arts, sponsoring the work of painters, architects and writers.

View of Florence, and its famous domed cathedral

It is often said the Renaissance began in the city state of **Florence**, which had grown wealthy during the medieval period through banking and the wool trade. As a **republic**, Florence was ruled by a collection of powerful families. The most powerful of these were the Medici, who supported the artist Michelangelo and the great Renaissance figure Leonardo da Vinci (see box). The dome of Florence Cathedral is one of the earliest examples of Renaissance architecture. It was designed by Filippo Brunelleschi and inspired in part by the Pantheon in Rome.

Another important Renaissance city was the Republic of **Venice**, which dominated Mediterranean trade routes and was the most prosperous city in Europe. A third Renaissance city was Milan. Though not a republic, Milan's ruling family, the Sforzas, transformed it into an artistic and cultural centre to rival Florence and Venice. In Rome, many more ancient statues and buildings were being uncovered. These inspired Renaissance sculptors and architects to copy their styles. This can be seen in the Corinthian columns at St Peter's Basilica in the Vatican, and statues such as Michelangelo's masterpiece *David*, completed in 1504.

Leonardo da Vinci

There were many great Renaissance philosophers, mathematicians, artists and inventers, but one man was all those things and more. His name was Leonardo da Vinci.

Born the illegitimate son of a poor farm girl in 1452, Leonardo began working for the Medici in Florence during his twenties. Aged 30 he moved to work for Ludovico Sforza in Milan. There he completed his masterpiece in 1499, a painting of the Last Supper on the refectory wall of the convent of Santa Maria delle Grazie.

Leonardo was also a great scientist and inventor, though many of his inventions were never made. His notebooks still exist today, and contain designs for a bicycle, helicopter, parachute and even a solar panel! They also reveal his obsessive struggle to find the fundamental patterns and rules that define human life, leading to his famous drawing of the perfectly proportioned 'Vitruvian Man'. It is sometimes difficult to believe that all of Leonardo's achievements and interests belonged to just one man.

Fact

Women artists were forbidden from using male models, making it difficult for them to create the same variety of works of art. However, several women did become major Renaissance painters. The most prominent was Artemisia Gentileschi, who had clients all over Europe including King Charles I of England.

Fact

Brunelleschi also developed the technique for creating **perspective** in artworks by using a vanishing point. Thanks to the use of perspective, Renaissance art is noticeably different to the flatter appearance of medieval paintings.

Completed by Raphael in 1504, this painting is an early example of perspective in Renaissance art

Check your understanding

1. How did the fall of Constantinople and the Crusades help spur the European Renaissance?
2. The growth of which institutions helped the spread of 'humanism' in medieval society?
3. Why were Italian city states so wealthy?
4. How did the artistic technique devised by Filippo Brunelleschi change Renaissance painting?
5. What were some of Leonardo da Vinci's accomplishments?

Global exploration

In medieval Europe, if a merchant wanted to trade directly with India or China, they faced a perilous overland journey lasting years. For this reason, few ever attempted it.

Goods from the Far East did reach Europe, but only after being passed from hand to hand along the network of routes known as the '**Silk Road**' through Central Asia. There was no direct trade, and this made such goods extremely expensive. By the time it arrived in Northern Europe, Chinese silk could be worn by only the wealthiest members of the nobility, and black pepper from India was an untold luxury.

Large parts of the Silk Road crossed through deserts, so camel trains were used to transport goods

Christopher Columbus

Christopher Columbus was an Italian sailor from Genoa with one big idea: finding a direct, seaborne route to trade with East Asia. Contrary to popular myth, it was commonly understood in medieval Europe that the world was round. By this logic, Columbus believed the Indian Ocean could be reached by sailing due west across the Atlantic. He was supported by King Ferdinand and Queen Isabella of Spain, who gave Columbus the money he required for a crew and three ships.

On 6 September 1492, Columbus set sail from the Canary Islands, led by his flagship the *Santa Maria*. Columbus calculated that Japan lay just 2400 miles away, and would take four weeks to reach. In fact, Japan was 7000 miles away from Europe, and a whole continent unknown to Europeans lay in between. Four weeks into the journey, Columbus and his men were running out of fresh water and about to turn back. But then, on 12 October, a member of Columbus's crew sighted land. It was the small Caribbean island of Guanahani. There, they found a peaceful **indigenous** people called the **Taíno**, who did not wear clothes, and spent their lives farming, fishing, and smoking rolled up leaves of a then unknown plant called tobacco. Columbus sailed on to the nearby island of Hispaniola, where he found indigenous people wearing small items of gold jewellery.

Columbus sailed back to Spain, bringing with him evidence of his discovery to show Ferdinand and Isabella: gold jewellery, chilli peppers, sweet potatoes, parrots, and nine captured indigenous people. Columbus's stories of a new land, and his hopes of finding greater reserves of gold, entranced the Spanish court.

Statue of Christopher Columbus in Barcelona, Spain

Contemporary engraving of Christopher Columbus landing at Hispaniola in 1492

With the support of Pope Alexander VI, Ferdinand and Isabella claimed ownership of all lands discovered across the Atlantic. The Portuguese King João II insisted that Spain should share the spoils, so in 1494 the **Treaty of Tordesillas** was signed. This extraordinary agreement drew a line down the globe running 370 leagues west of the Cape Verde Islands. Anything west of the line belonged to Spain, anything east of the line belonged to Portugal. To this day, most of South America speaks Spanish, aside from an eastern bulge jutting out into the Atlantic called Brazil, which speaks Portuguese.

Those explorers who followed Columbus would often describe the Americas as 'virgin' territory, meaning an untouched and uninhabited wilderness. This claim was used by Europeans to justify their conquest of land that was in fact inhabited by millions of native Americans. Besides seizing land through violence, the Europeans also brought with them diseases that the native population had no immunity to. Historians estimate that 90 per cent of the indigenous American population at the time of the European arrival died from new diseases such as measles, smallpox, malaria and tuberculosis. Nonetheless, descendants of indigenous people live throughout the Americas to this day.

Vasco da Gama

While Columbus had been sailing west, the Portuguese were attempting to reach Asia by sailing east – around Africa. East African ports had been trading with Asia for centuries, but for Europeans to do this, they had to sail around the treacherous **Cape of Good Hope** at the southern end of the African continent. Throughout the 15th century, Portuguese sailors travelled further and further down Africa's west coast, but very few were able to pass the Cape.

In 1497, the Portuguese explorer Vasco da Gama was chosen to lead an expedition to India. On 8 July his fleet of four ships and 170 men left Lisbon. Almost one year later, he landed at Calicut (now known as Kozhikode) in India, where they met the local king and exchanged European goods for a selection of Indian spices. After a horrendous journey home through the Indian monsoon, da Gama landed in Lisbon on 10 July 1499. Only 54 of his men had survived, but that did not matter to da Gama; he had become the first European to successfully sail to, and trade with, India.

In the years that followed, Portuguese sailors established a permanent trading post in Calicut and terrorised the Muslim merchants who had previously dominated Indian Ocean trade. A new age of trade, **colonies** and **empire** was emerging in Europe.

Fact

Columbus refused to believe that the Bible could have failed to mention an entire continent. Right up until his death in 1506, he insisted that he had simply found the outer islands of East Asia. Columbus's mistake can still be heard in the language we use today: a string of Caribbean islands are known as the 'West Indies' although this term is going out of use.

Portuguese explorer
Vasco da Gama

Check your understanding

1. What route did Christopher Columbus believe he could take to sail to East Asia?

2. What did Columbus find when he landed on the island of Guanahani?

3. What was decided between Spain and Portugal by the Treaty of Tordesillas?

4. What historic feat did Vasco da Gama achieve in 1499?

5. Why did so many of the indigenous people of the Americas die after Europeans made first contact?

Unit 6: Renaissance Europe
Print and astronomy

Under the influence of the Renaissance, new developments in technology and science led to great changes in the way that Europeans understood the world

The first important invention was the **printing press**. In medieval Europe, it could take a monk over a year to produce one handwritten Bible. For this reason, books were hugely expensive, and only the very wealthy or the very religious had access to them.

That was until Johannes Gutenberg, a metalworker from the German town of Mainz, started experimenting with printed text. The technology of printing with blocks of carved wood had arrived in Europe from China, but woodblock printing was time consuming and inefficient. Gutenberg's idea was to create equally sized individual letters out of metal that could be arranged and rearranged in a wooden frame to make whole pages of words, a technology known as '**movable-type printing**'. Gutenberg would then cover the metal type blocks with ink, and press onto them a sheet of paper, and then another, and then another.

Replica of an early printing press

In 1455, Gutenberg's **printing press** produced its first run of Bibles: 180 copies, each with 1286 pages. This started a **revolution**. By 1500, there were over 1000 printing presses in Western Europe, producing large numbers of books on religion, medicine, history, poetry, **astronomy** and Latin grammar, sold at prices that many more than just the wealthy could afford. New ideas could now spread to many more people at an unprecedented speed. It is no coincidence that the Reformation began just half a century after Gutenberg's revolutionary invention.

Astronomy

During the Renaissance, the ideas of the Greek astronomer Ptolemy were rediscovered. Ptolemy suggested that the heavenly bodies (sun, moon, planets and stars) revolved around the earth, something known as a '**geocentric**' theory of space. The Roman Catholic Church welcomed Ptolemy's theory, as it placed God and the earth at the centre of the universe.

Gunpowder

Gunpowder was invented in China, and first arrived in Europe during the 13th century. By the 16th century, gunpowder had conclusively spelled the end of medieval warfare. Faced with canon **bombardment**, Europe's most feared castles were defenceless – and even the famous city of walls of Constantinople, which had protected the Byzantines from invasion for 1000 years, crumbled after a sustained canon attack in 1453. Armed with a handgun, a lowly foot soldier could shoot dead a knight in shining armour.

However, a number of astronomers observed that the movement of the planets in the night sky was irregular, and they did not appear to orbit the earth. In 1543, Nicolaus Copernicus published a book called *The Revolution of the Heavenly Orbs*. In this book, Copernicus proposed a '**heliocentric**' theory, where the earth and the planets orbit the sun. The Catholic Church saw this as heresy, and banned Copernicus's book. But his troubling idea would not go away.

Galileo Galilei was a mathematics professor from Florence with an interest in astronomy. In 1609, he developed a new technology to observe the night sky: the telescope. Galileo openly supported Copernicus's heliocentric theory of the universe in his university lectures. In 1616 he was summoned to Rome where he was forced to deny his beliefs. Galileo was a committed Christian, so he agreed, but he could not sustain the lie. In 1632, he published *Dialogue concerning the Two Chief World Systems*. This book mocked the arguments of the Catholic Church, and explained Copernicus's heliocentric theory.

Now a frail old man, Galileo was once again summoned to Rome. This time, he was threatened with torture, and after a series of interrogations, Galileo denied that the earth revolved around the sun. For his remaining years, Galileo lived under house arrest, and died in 1642.

Galileo Galilei

Fact

The Catholic Church only formally ended their opposition to a heliocentric view of the universe in 1835.

Ferdinand Magellan

Global exploration continued during the 16th century. In September 1519, a Portuguese sailor working for the Spanish set sail for Indonesia, then known to the Portuguese as the Spice Islands, with five ships and around 265 men. Ferdinand Magellan plotted an audacious route heading west not east, intending to be the first European to sail around the tip of South America.

Magellan sailed towards Patagonia, where he claimed to encounter a race of giants, twice the size of Europeans. He then found a narrow channel leading to the other side of the continent. Freezing cold and beset with storms, the Magellan Strait, as it became known, is a dangerous route to sail. One ship sank, and another turned back. But after 38 days, Magellan and his men came out the other side, reaching an enormous ocean, which seemed calm in comparison. So they called it the Pacific Ocean, meaning 'peaceful'.

In March 1521, Magellan and his men reached the Philippines, where Magellan was killed by poisoned arrows during a battle with indigenous people. In September 1522, a single ship from Magellan's original expedition finally returned to Spain, with just 18 surviving men on board. However, they had earned their place in history as the first crew to **circumnavigate** the world.

Check your understanding

1. Why did the invention of the printing press make books cheaper and more efficient to produce?
2. Why did the invention of the printing press play an important role in the Reformation?
3. How did the use of gunpowder in Europe spell the end of medieval warfare?
4. How did the Pacific Ocean gain its name?
5. What did astronomers observe, which made them propose a heliocentric theory of space?

Unit 6: Renaissance Europe
Wars of religion

Following the Reformation (see Chapter 1, this unit), Western Europe became divided between Catholic and Protestant countries. A long series of religious wars lasted throughout the Early Modern period.

Catholics believed that the Pope was appointed by God as head of the Christian community on Earth. They thought that good Christians should always obey and respect the Church. Protestants rejected the authority of the Pope and placed much greater focus on the text of the Bible itself. They believed that faith alone, not obedience to the Church, could lead to salvation after death.

In the first half of the 16th century, Switzerland, England, Holland, Sweden and many of the small states and kingdoms of Germany became Protestant strongholds. France, Spain and the various states of Italy remained Catholic.

The Catholic Church was determined to oppose the rise of Protestantism, and so in 1545 Pope Paul III called a general council in the city of Trent, in northern Italy. The Council of Trent lasted until 1563 and launched the **Counter-Reformation**, a movement to strengthen Catholicism against the new form of Protestant Christianity. More powers were given to bishops, weekly attendance at mass (the Catholic service) was made compulsory, and some of the corrupt practices that had prompted Martin Luther's rebellion, such as the sale of indulgences (see Unit 1, Chapter 2), were ended.

Wars throughout Europe

The Holy Roman Emperor, Charles V, held power, in theory, over most of the German states. However, in many of them he held little power in practice. As a Catholic ruler, he was unable to prevent Protestantism spreading through much of Germany. In 1555, at a council called the Diet of Augsburg, Charles was forced to agree that the religion of each state should be the same as the religion of its ruler. This meant accepting that many German states would remain Protestant.

John Calvin (1509–64)

Calvinism

One particularly strict form of Protestantism was developed by John Calvin, a Frenchman who came to dominate the city-state of Geneva in Switzerland. Calvin believed that the only people favoured by God were the 'Elect', a tiny minority of morally pure individuals. Only the Elect were destined to be saved from damnation after death. Under Calvin, the death penalty was imposed for a range of offences including blasphemy, adultery and witchcraft. **Calvinism** influenced Protestant groups throughout Europe, including the Puritans in England and the Church in Scotland.

In France there were nine religious wars between 1562 and 1598, a period when France was dominated by Queen Catherine de Medici. They were fought to suppress the French Protestants, who were known as **Huguenots**. These wars were about more than religion: they were also struggles for power between France's nobles, who were often Protestant, and the monarchy, which was Catholic. Great violence was committed by both sides – most famously the St Bartholomew's Day Massacre in 1572, when thousands of Huguenots in Paris were slaughtered by royal troops. Eventually, King Henry IV came to the throne in 1589 and attempted to end the religious wars. The Huguenots were granted special protections, including the possession of fortified towns where the king had no authority. However, most French people remained Catholic.

The St Bartholomew's Day Massacre, painted by Francois Dubois, a French Huguenot painter, around 1580

In the **Low Countries**, religious warfare eventually led to the creation of two modern nations. The whole region had been part of the empire of Charles V, but in 1556 he passed it on to his son Philip II, the new King of Spain. Local nobles did not trust Philip, and in 1566 they began fighting for their independence. The conflict, usually known as the Dutch Revolt, lasted for over 80 years. It ended with the Spanish armies keeping control of the mostly Catholic and French-speaking southern provinces, while the mostly Protestant and Dutch-speaking northern provinces became independent. The south would later become Belgium; the north became the United Provinces, today known as the Netherlands.

The most destructive of Europe's wars of religion was the **Thirty Years' War**, which lasted from 1618 to 1648. This was a complex struggle for power in central Europe, fought between many different states and kingdoms. Most of the fighting took place in German states, but the war also spread to France and the Low Countries. It began when Holy Roman Emperor Ferdinand II attempted to impose Catholicism on his Bohemian (Czech) territories, and Protestant nobles rose in rebellion. However, like many of the religious wars, the Thirty Years' War was not only about religion. Many historians see it as a struggle for power and territory between the Habsburg family, who ruled the Holy Roman Empire, and the kings of France – both of which were Catholic powers.

The Thirty Years' War ended with the Peace of Westphalia in 1648. The Holy Roman Empire lost much of its power, while France was left as the strongest nation in Europe. Europe's wars of religion were not over, but the Peace of Westphalia brought the worst of these conflicts to an end.

> ### Fact
>
> In some parts of Germany, the population is thought to have declined by over two-thirds during the Thirty Years' War, due to a combination of warfare, starvation and disease.

Check your understanding

1. What were the main features of the Counter-Reformation?
2. What beliefs did John Calvin and his followers hold?
3. What was the outcome of the religious wars in France?
4. How did the United Provinces come to be independent from Spain?
5. Why do many historians argue that the Early Modern wars of religion were not only about religion?

The witch craze

In Early Modern Europe, widespread fear of witches led to a centuries-long series of witch-hunts. Historians call this the 'witch craze'.

Throughout medieval history, there had always been women suspected of witchcraft. Often, they were healers or fortune-tellers, known as 'cunningfolk', who were respected and valued within their communities – even if they were sometimes also treated with suspicion. However, from Renaissance times onwards, attitudes to witchcraft became much more fearful. It became common to believe that witches were people who worshipped the Devil. This made witchcraft a form of **heresy**, meaning disobedience to God's commands. Witchcraft was made illegal in most parts of Europe during the 16th century, including in England in 1542.

It was thought that witches were given supernatural powers by the Devil in exchange for carrying out his commands. It was said that witches could fly, often on broomsticks, and that they performed secret rituals together in groups called covens. These rituals might include killing and even eating kidnapped children. A witch was said to be accompanied by a demonic companion called a familiar, who took an animal form such as a cat or a toad. Many people believed that witches could use their magic to cause the death of those who offended or angered them.

In the Early Modern period, thousands of people throughout Europe, most of them women, were accused of witchcraft by their neighbours or by Church authorities. Very often they were tortured into confessing their guilt. They were usually executed by hanging or by burning at the stake. Most witch trials took place over the hundred years between 1550 and 1650, though the persecution of witches continued long afterwards. In Britain, the last person to be executed for witchcraft was Janet Horne, in 1727. In total, between 50 000 and 60 000 people were executed for witchcraft, and around 80 per cent of them were women.

> **Fact**
>
> Some people dedicated their careers to hunting witches. Matthew Hopkins was an Englishman who served as 'Witchfinder General' in the 1640s, during the English Civil War. He is believed to have been responsible for the execution of over a hundred people accused of witchcraft.

Woodcut print from *Malleus Maleficarum*, the witch-hunting handbook of the medieval period

Malleus Maleficarum

Around 1486, a book called ***Malleus Maleficarum***, meaning 'Hammer of the Witches', was written by Heinrich Kraemer, a German university professor. In his book, Kraemer argued that witches were everywhere, and gave detailed instructions for identifying them and killing them. Though it was thought that men could also be witches, this book's heavily misogynistic tone put the focus firmly on women. *Malleus Maleficarum* came to be accepted as the standard guide to combatting witchcraft and it played a major role in causing the fear of witches to spread. For almost 200 years it was the second highest-selling book in Europe, after the Bible!

Explaining the witch craze

Historians continue to debate the question of why Europeans become so much more suspicious of witchcraft in the Early Modern period. Some believe this fear was linked to the Reformation, which directly preceded the witch-hunting craze, as witches were pursued in both Catholic and Protestant countries. Some historians suggest it arose from competition between Catholic and Protestant faiths to win worshippers round to their form of Christianity. In this competitive atmosphere, persecuting witches was a very visible way for churches to combat Satan's evil.

Other historians argue that accusations of witchcraft arose from jealousy between neighbours or from prejudices against women. Most women accused of witchcraft were single, elderly women, often widows, and without close relatives in their communities. When other people in their villages suffered misfortunes, such as illness, bad harvests, or the death of crops or livestock, it was easy to blame these women by accusing them of causing the trouble with magic. Married men who had affairs also often accused women of using witchcraft to enchant them so that women could be blamed instead of them. Other women who did not keep to their traditional social roles, such as widows who did not remarry and women who performed abortions, were also targeted.

English 'Witchfinder General' Matthew Hopkins, who hunted 'witches' between 1644 and and 1647

Most broadly, this was also a time of rapid social, political and religious change. Some scholars believe that the witch craze happened simply because ordinary people felt that the world was out of their control and they wanted somebody to blame.

The Salem witches

The most famous set of witch trials in history did not take place in Europe, but in the village of Salem, Massachusetts, in one of Britain's colonies on the coast of North America. In January 1692, two young girls in the village named Elizabeth Parris (also known as Betty) and Abigail Williams began having fits. Betty's father, Samuel Parris, was the local minister and decided that the girls must be under a spell, and pressed them to say who was bewitching them. Betty and Abigail eventually accused three local women of witchcraft. All three of the accused were low status and isolated individuals: a beggar named Sarah Good; an elderly woman named Sarah Osborne, who had recently been ridiculed by the community for having an affair with a servant; and a woman named Tituba, who was enslaved by the Parris family.

After Tituba was forced into confessing to witchcraft, describing in detail her activities such as riding on broomsticks, the community decided there must be more witches among them. Soon, other young girls began exhibiting the same symptoms as Betty and Abigail, and accusing more people of witchcraft. Those who were accused were usually either widely disliked, or family enemies of their accusers. In the summer of 1692, a total of 20 men and women were executed as witches in Salem, 19 by hanging and one by being pressed to death by heavy stones.

Check your understanding

1. How did Early Modern attitudes to witchcraft differ from medieval attitudes?

2. How did the *Malleus Maleficarum* contribute to the witch craze?

3. What beliefs were commonly held about witches?

4. Why were 19 women hanged in Salem, Massachusetts, in 1692?

5. How have modern historians attempted to explain the witch craze?

Unit 6: Renaissance Europe
Knowledge organiser

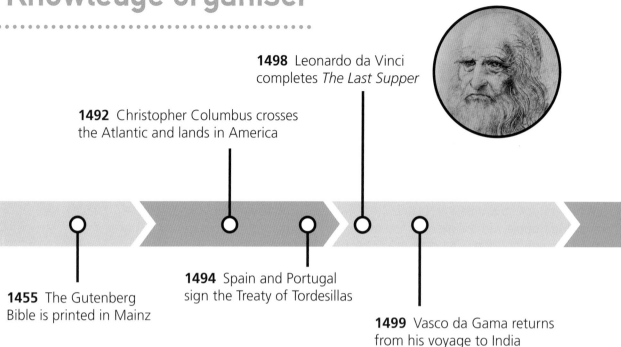

1498 Leonardo da Vinci completes *The Last Supper*

1492 Christopher Columbus crosses the Atlantic and lands in America

1455 The Gutenberg Bible is printed in Mainz

1494 Spain and Portugal sign the Treaty of Tordesillas

1499 Vasco da Gama returns from his voyage to India

Key vocabulary

Astronomy The science of studying extraterrestrial objects, and the universe

Bombardment The act of attacking a place with missiles continuously

Calvinism Strict form of Protestantism developed by John Calvin and associated with Geneva

Cape of Good Hope The southern end of Africa, notorious for its stormy weather and rough seas

Circumnavigate To sail around something, often used to mean sailing around the world

City state A political system where a single city governs itself and its surrounding territories

Classical Relating to the art, culture or history of Ancient Greece and Rome

Colony A country or area under the political control of a foreign country

Counter-Reformation Catholic fight back against the spread of Protestantism in Europe

Empire A group of countries or states presided over by a single ruler

Florence Italian city state and banking centre where the Renaissance was said to have begun

Geocentric A system in astronomy where the earth is at the centre of the universe

Heliocentric A system in astronomy where the Sun is at the centre of the universe, or solar system

Heresy Disobedience to the official form of a religion

Huguenots Term usually given to French Protestants

Humanism A system of thought which concentrates on the human realm, often in place of religion

Indigenous A person born in, or historically associated with, a particular country or region

Low Countries Common term for Belgium, Luxembourg and the Netherlands

Malleus Maleficarum Meaning 'Hammer of the Witches', a very influential guide to identifying and destroying witches

Movable-type printing A system of printing that uses and rearranges individual letters and punctuation

Patron Someone who gives financial support to a person or institution, most often an artist

Perspective A method in art of depicting three-dimensional objects, often using a vanishing point

Printing Press A revolutionary invention that enabled the mass production of books

Enquiry Question: Was life in Renaissance Europe dominated by reason or by superstition?

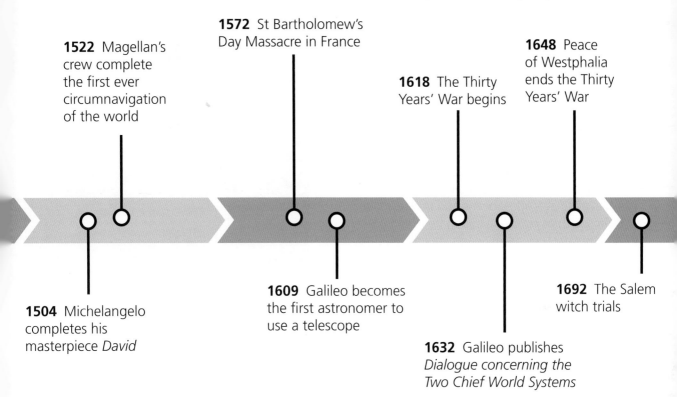

1522 Magellan's crew complete the first ever circumnavigation of the world

1572 St Bartholomew's Day Massacre in France

1618 The Thirty Years' War begins

1648 Peace of Westphalia ends the Thirty Years' War

1504 Michelangelo completes his masterpiece *David*

1609 Galileo becomes the first astronomer to use a telescope

1632 Galileo publishes *Dialogue concerning the Two Chief World Systems*

1692 The Salem witch trials

Key vocabulary

Renaissance Literally meaning 'rebirth', a period of cultural flourishing in Early Modern Europe

Republic A state where the ruler is not a monarch, but comes from among the people

Revolution A change which means that nothing will ever be the same again

Silk Road An ancient overground trade route that linked East Asia with the West

Taíno The indigenous people of the Caribbean, wiped out by European diseases

Thirty Years' War Most destructive of Europe's religious wars, a complex struggle fought mostly in what is now Germany

Treaty of Tordesillas A treaty that divided the New World between Spain and Portugal

Venice City in northern Italy that dominated Mediterranean trade during the medieval period

Key people

John Calvin Christian reformer whose strict interpretation of Protestantism became widely influential

Christopher Columbus Explorer who crossed the Atlantic and claimed the land he encountered for Spain

Ferdinand Magellan Portuguese explorer who was the first person to circumnavigate the world

Filippo Brunelleschi Renaissance architect and artist who pioneered the use of perspective

Galileo Galilei Italian astronomer who supported a heliocentric theory of the universe

Johannes Gutenberg German publisher who introduced movable-type printing to Europe

Leonardo da Vinci Renaissance genius who painted *The Last Supper*

Vasco da Gama The first European to establish an overseas trading route with India

Maya city states

For thousands of years, the Americas were home to a vast array of civilisations and cultures. In **Mesoamerica**, one of the oldest and longest enduring were the **Maya**.

The Maya people settled in Mesoamerica around 2000 BCE. City states began to emerge from 300 CE in the tropical jungles of the Yucatán peninsula of Mexico and modern Belize, Guatemala and Honduras. The Maya ate avocados, beans and **maize** as well as dishes such as *poc chuc* (marinated charcoal-roasted meat). They drank warm chocolate drinks and smoked tobacco leaves from pipes made of hollow bones.

The ruins of Palenque, Yucatán, Mexico

The Maya took much of their culture from the earlier Olmec civilisation, which is famous for the sculpting of huge stone heads. At the height of the Maya civilisation, large stone buildings, including impressive monuments and pyramid temples, were built. Many of these survive today at sites such as Tikal, Chichen Itza, Copan, Uxmal, Lamanai and Palenque. There were more than 40 Maya cities with populations of between 5000 and 50 000, giving a total population of perhaps 2 million inhabitants.

Each of the Maya city states had a separate ruling family who either negotiated dynastic alliances with rival rulers or attempted to conquer them in armed conflict. The priesthood acted as important advisors for Maya rulers and had to undergo rigorous training. They held high prestige within Maya society for memorising history, poetry and songs, as well as their proficiency in the Mayan language, calendars, medicine and astronomy.

The Maya developed sophisticated mathematical and astronomical methods that allowed the development of advanced irrigation systems for farming in the jungles and a complex calendar for timekeeping. An important feature of Maya education was an emphasis on character as well as knowledge: parents were expected to teach their children mental strength, compassion, loyalty to the community and self-control.

Fact

The Maya used multiple calendars to record time. The Calendar Round was a 52-year cycle using a combination of 260 days. The Long Count was used to record important births, royal events and battle triumphs. It counted every individual day for 5125 years from what the Maya believed to be the day of creation, 11 August 3114 BCE, to 21 December 2012.

Note on pronunciation

The predominant languages of ancient Mesoamerica are Mayan and **Nahuatl**, both of which are still spoken today. They were originally written using pictures called glyphs, but during the 16th century the languages were transcribed into the Latin alphabet. Words can be read phonetically, though it should be noted that an 'x' is pronounced 'sh'.

Maya mythology

The **Popol Vuh** is an important Maya mythological narrative that was preserved through oral history until it was written down in the 16th century. The stories in the Popol Vuh explain the Maya belief that there have been phases of creation and destruction for millennia, with many struggles between different gods and heroes before the present world. The creator gods brought objects into being from the emptiness of space by talking to each other – whatever they said was created. The current world was created after a great flood wiped away failed attempts to create humans out of mud and wood.

In one story, the arrogant and powerful bird demon Vucub-Caquix (Seven Macaw) pretended to be the sun and moon and had to be defeated by the Hero Twins. He was shot down from a tree with a blowpipe and stripped of his powers. The Hero Twins were later summoned to play a ball game (see box) in the underworld by the Lords of Xibalba (Place of Fright), who presided over various gruesome challenges they had to undergo. The names of the Lords of Xibalba tell us how terrifying the Maya believed the underworld to be: some of the translations of their names include 'Flying Scab', 'Gathered Blood', 'Pus Demon' and 'Skull Staff'.

To honour their gods, the Maya built huge stone pyramids at the centre of their cities. These symbolised the centre of the universe and were the focus for rituals that sometimes included human sacrifice. Before their death, sacrificial victims were treated with great respect and ceremony – their handprints were painted on doorways and the **tzompantli** (skull rack) acknowledged all those who had given their lives to the gods. While a full human sacrifice may have been rare, bloodletting was a common practice (as it was in Europe). Human blood was known as 'precious liquid' (**chalchiuatl** in Nahuatl) so it was considered a privilege to give your own blood to the gods. Jaguar claws, stingray spines, cactus spikes, **obsidian** blades or strings threaded with thorns were used to make the offerings.

Carvings of the skull rack at Chichen Itza, Mexico

Ancient ballgame

In many Mesoamerican cities there are ball courts for playing **ullamaliztli**. Players had to use only their knees, elbows and hips to bounce a solid rubber ball weighing up to 4 kg across a line or through narrow rings high on the walls. While the game was sometimes played for fun, and possibly even by children and women, city states could also settle political disputes with victory or defeat in the game.

Check your understanding

1. Which modern countries did the Maya city states cover?
2. How were Maya city states ruled?
3. What does the Popol Vuh tell us about Mayan creation beliefs?
4. What heroic acts did the Hero Twins achieve?
5. Why did the Maya use sacrifice and bloodletting rituals?

Unit 7: The Americas
Rise of the Aztecs

In the 1200s, a North American tribe called the Mexica migrated into Mesoamerica. They would eventually become the most powerful group in the region.

Guided by their war god Huitzilopochtli (Hummingbird Left), the Mexica roamed southwards for almost a century, eventually arriving at **Lake Texcoco**. According to myth, it was here that they saw an eagle on a prickly cactus holding a writhing serpent, indicating that this was where they should build their city.

By 1325, the Mexica had established the city of **Tenochtitlan** and were beginning to expand their control across Mesoamerica, in the regions of modern Mexico. The Mexica traced their North American homeland to a town called Aztlan, so their civilisation later became known as the **Aztecs**.

Aztec rule

The first recorded ruler of the Aztecs dates from around 1376, when Acamapichtli was elected **tlatoani** ('speaker'). The tlatoani marked their status with colourful feathered headdresses, elaborate capes and rich jewellery made of gold, rock crystal, turquoise and jade.

Around 1428, the Aztecs formed a series of political marriage alliances with other tribes, which were formalised as the Triple Alliance of Tenochtitlan, Texcoco and Tlacopan. From this point, the Aztecs became the strongest and most centralised state in Mesoamerica, expanding their control and receiving **tribute** payments from those they conquered or formed alliances with. The empire was split into 38 administrative provinces, with representatives from Tenochtitlan sent to live in each. They ensured tribute was collected on time and acted as judges in local disputes. Permanent military garrisons were also built at key locations.

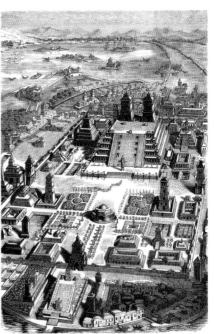

Artist's reconstruction of the great city of Tenochtitlan

Life in Tenochtitlan

Tenochtitlan was an enormous city with perhaps more than 100 000 inhabitants, rivalling Constantinople in size. Sitting on an island in Lake Texcoco, life in Tenochtitlan was made possible by extraordinary feats of engineering. Giant causeways linked the city to the mainland. Artificial 'floating gardens' called **chinampas** used careful irrigation to grow crops on little islands on the lake. Canals filtered through the city with canoes full of exotic products destined for the market square, where you could buy luxury goods such as golden jewellery, jaguar skins and colourful parrot feathers, as well as all kinds of foodstuffs from toasted corn, tomatoes, squash and stuffed tortillas to chilli peppers, sweet potatoes, cacao beans and vanilla pods.

Some city states such as **Tlaxcala** remained independent territories. However, for this privilege they were forced to participate in the Flower Wars. These were ritualised battles held at pre-selected locations on pre-determined dates with the aim of capturing as many of the enemy as possible (some of whom would be used in rituals as sacrificial victims). They also served to keep warriors in top fighting form; if a warrior from the lower class carried out 20 or more deeds of remarkable bravery, they became a **quauhpilli** (Eagle Noble). This entitled them to wear special outfits, join elite warrior orders and practise **polygamy** like the nobility.

Aztec society also used slavery, with women who had been captured as prisoners of war often given as tribute payments. In times of desperation, poor families could sell relatives into slavery, and it was also a punishment for committing crimes. However, enslaved people could buy their freedom and their children were considered free.

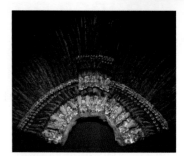

Aztec-era headdress, said to have belonged to Aztec emperor Moctezum a II

Aztec religion

In Aztec religion, the creator gods Quetzalcoatl (Plumed Serpent) and Tezcatlipoca (Smoking Mirror) had to defeat a monster goddess named Tlaltecuhtli (Giver and Devourer of Life) for the cosmos to prosper. They pulled apart her body to create the earth and sky and made new humans out of maize dough. But Tlaltecuhtli was angry at being unwillingly sacrificed and demanded blood for the world of the Fifth Sun to continue. A humble god named Nanahuatzin (Full of Sores) had the courage to jump into the flames of a sacred fire to light the Fifth Sun. A jaguar and an eagle followed his example, gaining their black markings and becoming symbols of fearlessness and power.

Aztec priest performing the sacrificial offering of a living human's heart to the war god Huitzilopochtli

Sacrifice in times of extreme danger was therefore considered a brave act, and an essential duty for the continued functioning of the cosmos. The Great Pyramid of Tenochtitlan was built as the focus of religious ritual, including human sacrifice. It is unclear how often it was performed (and was exaggerated by Europeans for centuries). However, it seems that as the Aztec empire expanded, what had been a rare sacred act may have been turned into a way to inspire fear and maintain control through sacrificing prisoners of war.

The Aztecs believed that the way you died rather than your achievements determined where you would spend the afterlife. Those who were sacrificed, died in battle or died giving birth had the greatest honour in the afterlife, helping the gods to move the sun through the sky. Those who died by drowning or diseases related to water went to the kingdom of flowers and fountains with the water gods.

> ### Fact
> The Aztecs were one of the first people in the world to ensure compulsory state financed education for nearly all children, regardless of gender or class in society.

Check your understanding

1. Why was Tenochtitlan such an impressive city?

2. What was the role of the tlatoani?

3. How did the Triple Alliance maintain Aztec power?

4. Why were the Flower Wars initiated by the Aztecs?

5. How did Aztec religious beliefs inspire bravery in the people?

The Inca empire

While the Aztecs established power over Mesoamerica, the Inca built the largest empire in South America during the same period.

Manco Cápac

The legendary founder of the **Inca** dynasty was Manco Cápac. He was said to have been the child of the sun god Inti and the moon goddess Mama Killa. Around 1100 CE, he led his people through the sacred valley of **Lake Titicaca** and founded what was to become the Inca capital of **Cusco** further to the north.

In the 15th century under Pachacuti and Tupac, the Inca empire expanded dramatically. It eventually covered an area of over 4000 square kilometres, incorporating parts of modern-day Peru, Chile, Bolivia, Ecuador, Colombia and Argentina. This landscape ranged from plains and deserts to mountains and rainforests. The **Andean** cultures were forcefully united as never before with the creation of a vast road network for rapid communication and manoeuvring troops. A state cult to Inti was imposed across the empire, with the Inca emperor himself personifying the god.

State organisation

The Inca emperor led a remarkably powerful central government that redistributed labour and goods across the empire. The emperor's title of 'Sapa Inca' ('Only Inca') showed his primary importance in the running of the state.

Panoramic view of Machu Picchu, a royal retreat located on a 2430-metre mountain ridge in southern Peru. The site was abandoned by the 16th century

All adult men had to serve compulsory public service called **mit'a** for a certain number of days each year, usually to complete construction projects such as roads, bridges, fortifications and terraces. Due to the empire's mountainous landscape, the Inca built terraces on hillsides to extend the amount of flat land available for farming. Key crops were maize and potatoes, while llamas were a vital resource for providing transport, clothing, milk and meat. Two-thirds of all goods produced in a community were collected by the army and state officials, who redistributed them across all levels of society and provided reserves in times of famine.

Another form of government control was the deliberate transfer of populations. This could be used to shift groups loyal to the Inca to frontier provinces, break up rebellious groups, or move individuals to different areas for agricultural purposes. For example, from the late 15th century, the emperor Huayna Capac relocated 14 000 people to the Cochabamba valley in Bolivia to increase **coca** and maize production.

Several thousand women from across the empire became **Aclla Cuna** ('Chosen Women') and lived in temple convents under a vow of chastity. They were chosen at age 8 to 10 for their beauty, intelligence and talents from among the villages across the empire and remained in the temple precinct for 6–7 years. They maintained a sacred fire, wove clothes for the emperor and prepared ritual food and **chicha** beer for festivals. After this time, they became either sacrificial victims, imperial concubines or wives of nobles.

Quipu

There was no written language among any of the Andean civilisations before the Spanish conquest. Instead, teachers known as **amautas** ('wise ones') were responsible for memorising and reciting legends and history, and keeping records to pass on to the next generation. To help them with this, a system of knots in strings called **quipu** was used. The different colours of cotton and llama wool as well as the direction the knots were tied in could be 'read' by the amautas.

Religion in Cusco

All roads in the Inca empire led to Cusco, the centre of the Inca empire. The plan of the city resembled the shape of a crouching puma. In the centre of the city were the main palace of the emperor and the most important temple – the **Coricancha**. This enclosure housed a temple to Inti covered in gold leaf representing the 'sweat of the sun' and a temple to Mama Killa covered in silver leaf, the 'tears of the moon'.

16th-century wood cut showing quipu, the Inca method of recording information by knotting threads of different lengths and colours

Radiating out from the Coricancha were over 40 ceque lines that led to 328 **huacas** (sacred sites) across the empire. For the **Capacocha** ceremony, boys and girls were selected from across the Inca empire to walk the ceque lines to Cusco, be sanctified by priests in the Coricancha, and then walk back to their villages to be left to die on sacred mountaintops. Although this ceremony was performed rarely, it was designed to renew and reaffirm the bond between the Inca state and provincial peoples, emphasising the unquestionable control of the Inca overlords and connect the Inca people to their gods.

The Coricancha was also where royal mummies were kept. Mummification was important throughout the Andean cultures as a way to connect with all levels of the cosmos. Pachamama was the powerful goddess of the earth and the four key principles of life – Earth, Water, Sun and Moon – were held together in an endless cycle. Nature was seen as a living, sacred being that needed to be cared for and humans were just one group among all living things. Mummified bodies were treated as living family members, brought out to watch the sun rise and be consulted on everyday concerns as well as participating in festivals. **Shamans** ate coca leaves and cactus buds to give hallucinogenic visions and speak to them.

Fact

The earliest deliberately mummified bodies found in the Andes are from the Chinchorro culture in northern Chile, dating to around 5050 BCE. These predate the earliest Egyptian mummies by around 2000 years.

Check your understanding

1. What was the legend about how the Inca royal dynasty was founded?
2. How did the state organise labour and goods during the Inca empire?
3. What role did the Aclla Cuna play in Inca society?
4. Why was the Coricancha important?
5. What was the most powerful way the Incas exerted control in their empire?

Unit 7: The Americas
Cortés and the Aztecs

After Christopher Columbus crossed the Atlantic and encountered a 'New World' in 1492, the Spanish king authorised **conquistadors** to create a new Spanish empire by colonising the Americas.

Hernán Cortés first sailed to the Americas in 1504 aged 18, where he took part in the conquest of Cuba. He was rewarded with land and enslaved people, but saw an opportunity to gain more power and wealth if he led his own expedition on the American mainland. Ignoring the commands of Governor Diego Velázquez to remain in Cuba, Cortés set sail in February 1519 with 11 ships carrying just over 500 men, a small number of horses, guns, cannons and war dogs.

Moctezuma II confronts Cortés

At the time of Cortés' arrival, Moctezuma II had been tlatoani in Tenochtitlan since 1502, and his empire covered around 200 000 square kilometres of Mesoamerica. When messengers informed Moctezuma that people from far-off lands were travelling through Mexico, he hoped that by offering them tribute the foreigners would be satisfied and leave. However, when Cortés received gold and gifts, it only fuelled his desire to find more.

Artist's impression of the meeting between the Spanish conquistador Hernán Cortés and the Aztec emperor Moctezuma II in Tenochtitlan, 1519. Malintzin can be seen to the right of Cortés.

Soon the conquistadors reached Tlaxcala, the determined enemies of the Aztecs (see Chapter 2, this unit). An enslaved woman called Malintzin who spoke Nahuatl and Mayan fluently was able to convince the Tlaxcalans to ally with Cortés and join his assault on Tenochtitlan. She proved to be a crucial aid to the conquistadors, learning Spanish and acting as their interpreter during their negotiations.

As Cortés approached Tenochtitlan on 8 November 1519, Moctezuma welcomed him as a fellow monarch in a grand display of Aztec diplomacy. He invited Cortés and his army into the city with a parade and gifts, and led them into his palace where they could rest after their journey.

Rebellion and destruction

Despite Moctezuma's hospitality, Cortés took him hostage. Cortés believed that with Malintzin's interpretations, he could negotiate the Aztecs' submission to the Spanish king and rule indirectly through Moctezuma. Cortés kept Moctezuma under strict control, forcing him to issue commands to gather as much gold as possible and not rebel.

In April 1520, 13 ships sent by Governor Velázquez landed in Mexico with orders to arrest Cortés and bring him back to Cuba. Cortés left Tenochtitlan to convince Velázquez's troops to join his expedition. However, in Cortés's absence, the men he left behind in Tenochtitlan became more fearful of Aztec rebellion and took brutal defensive action, massacring hundreds of unarmed Aztec nobles, warriors and priests during a religious festival.

By the time Cortés returned in June, the Aztecs were in open conflict with the conquistadors. Cortés forced the captive Moctezuma to make a speech, urging co-operation with the Spanish, but Moctezuma had lost all authority and was killed. The Spanish tried to escape in the night with as much gold as they could carry, but the Aztecs raised the alarm and hundreds of Spaniards were killed or sacrificed to the gods in what became known as La Noche Triste ('The Night of Sorrows').

It looked like everything was over for Cortés and his men. However, although the Europeans had been repelled, they had left behind an invisible enemy: smallpox. The indigenous peoples of Mesoamerica had no immunity and tens of thousands died.

In April 1521, Cortés returned with an enlarged invasion force, including tens of thousands of Tlaxcalan allies, 13 ships and a few cannons. Although the Aztecs defended their city against a siege for 93 days, their obsidian spear tips and arrowheads simply shattered against the metal armour of the conquistadors. Tenochtitlan was razed to the ground.

Post-conquest life

For the Aztecs, life after European conquest was characterised by forced conversion to Christianity and the destruction of indigenous records and monuments. The Great Pyramid of Tenochtitlan was dismantled, and the stones were used to build a Catholic cathedral on its foundations. Tenochtitlan was renamed Mexico City, the capital of the colony 'New Spain'.

Some of the Aztec nobility kept positions of wealth and status by working with the Spanish, collecting tribute and intermarrying with the invaders. Yet further epidemics of European diseases killed up to 90 per cent of the indigenous population. So great was the loss of life that enslaved people from Africa and the Philippines were shipped to Mexico to work in their place.

> **Fact**
>
> A popular story in the 16th century was that the Aztecs submitted to Cortés because they believed he was their god Quetzalcoatl. Many historians think this story was invented by the Spanish to make the Aztecs seem blinded by a false religion, so justifying their conquest and the Aztecs' defeat.

Illustration from a 16th-century manuscript showing Malintzin negotiating an alliance with the Tlaxcalans.

> **Fact**
>
> In 1550–01, the Spanish king held the Council of Valladolid to discuss the legal questions of indigenous human rights in the colonies. Although imperialism intensified during this period, the debate itself showed there were growing concerns about the enslavement of indigenous Americans and establishing laws to protect them.

Check your understanding

1. Why did Hernán Cortés go to Mexico?
2. What did Malintzin do?
3. What happened to Moctezuma?
4. How was Cortés able to attack Tenochtitlan again after La Noche Triste?
5. What was the most significant reason for the defeat of the Aztecs?

Pizarro and the Inca

Stories of Hernán Cortés' successful conquest of Mexico prompted other conquistadors, such as Francisco Pizarro, to seek glory and fortune elsewhere in the Americas.

Pizarro led expeditions along the Pacific coast in 1524 and 1526, but they failed due to strong winds and concerns over sightings of an organised warrior civilisation. However, Pizarro was determined to succeed. It was said that he drew a line in the sand and challenged his men to either join him in the search for riches in Peru or return to poverty in Panama. In 1531, Pizarro's third expedition of some 200 conquistadors landed on the coast of modern-day Ecuador.

Inca civil war

Before Pizarro's arrival in South America, the epidemics of diseases such as smallpox and measles that had ravaged the Aztecs (see Chapter 4, this unit) had also reached the Inca empire. After the Inca emperor Huayna Capac died from disease in 1524, a civil war broke out between two of his sons, Huascar and Atahualpa. After many battles, Atahualpa's forces finally reached Cusco in April 1532, where he captured Huascar and killed his supporters. So, before the conquistadors even arrived, European influences had divided what previously had been a united empire.

Atahualpa meets Pizarro

After defeating his brother, Atahualpa and his 80 000-strong army were resting in the town of Cajamarca. It was here that he received news of foreigners travelling through his lands. However, Pizarro's men seemed too small a force to be threatening, so Atahualpa invited them to visit his camp.

On 16 November 1532, Atahualpa was carried on a litter dressed in his finest clothes and a golden headdress to meet the visitors. His warriors laid down their weapons as a sign of trust and a golden cup of chicha beer was offered to Pizarro and his men. However, the Spanish poured the chicha onto the ground. Then Friar Vicente de Valverde stepped forward brandishing a Bible and crucifix to tell the Inca to repent and convert to Christianity. Atahualpa was unimpressed and threw the Bible to the floor, not realising its significance to the Spaniards.

Unknown to Atahualpa, Pizarro had hidden cannons and cavalry, which were now unleashed onto the unarmed Inca forces. The Inca had never fought horses or guns, so panic and confusion followed, allowing Pizarro to seize Atahualpa and hold him hostage. As the Spanish began to loot the Inca camp, Atahualpa noticed their lust for precious metals and offered a ransom for his freedom. He said that within two months he could fill the room he was being held hostage in once with gold and twice with silver. Atahualpa was true to his word – the conquistadors melted

Fact

Pizarro was 31 years old when he sailed to the 'New World' in 1509, and he became one of the first Europeans to reach the Pacific Ocean while exploring Panama. It was there that he heard stories of rich cities to the south.

Fact

On European maps, the Americas were named after the Italian explorer Amerigo Vespucci who sailed south along the coast of Brazil in 1502, proving the existence of a whole continent rather than an island as Columbus had assumed.

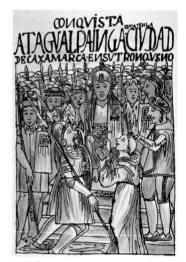

The first meeting, in 1532, of Francisco Pizarro and Atahualpa, the last Inca king of Peru

beautiful pieces of Inca craftsmanship into approximately 6000 kg of gold ingots and 12 000 kg of silver ingots to take back to Spain.

When Atahualpa demanded to be set free, Pizarro's fellow commander Diego de Almagro remained fearful that Atahualpa's generals would regroup and attack. He recommended that Atahualpa be executed. Pizarro and Almagro acted as judges in a mock trial, accusing Atahualpa of assassinating his brother Huascar, refusing to convert to Christianity, and plotting against the Spanish Crown. Atahualpa was sentenced to death on 26 July 1533. To avoid being burned at the stake (so that his body could be preserved for the afterlife), Atahualpa pleaded to be baptised and then strangled. Pizarro agreed, then marched his forces to the Inca capital of Cusco.

Artist's impression of the last Inca Emperor, Atahualpa, as he converted to Christianity to avoid being burned at the stake

Inca resistance

In Cusco, Pizarro installed Atahualpa's 18-year-old brother as Manco II to perform ceremonial duties and keep resistance low while the Spanish consolidated their invasion. Manco was a puppet ruler who was tortured to reveal the location of more Inca riches. In 1536, Manco played to the greed of the Spanish and told them that he needed to leave Cusco to perform a religious ceremony and would bring back a golden statue. Instead, he escaped and summoned perhaps as many as 200 000 warriors to lead a siege on Cusco. Manco's siege almost succeeded, but ended when Almagro arrived with reinforcements.

Manco and his army retreated to the remote **Vilcabamba** valley, high in the Andes mountains. Here, he founded a Neo-Inca state that launched a **guerrilla** campaign against Spanish garrisons and expeditions, making travel unsafe. Meanwhile in Cusco, Pizarro and Almagro had become bitter enemies in a civil war for control of the colony and were both assassinated. Then, in 1544, Manco was assassinated by Spanish soldiers that had infiltrated Vilcabamba. Spanish domination of the South American continent intensified, though rebellions under Manco's son Túpac Amaru continued until 1572.

Resisting colonisation

As with the Aztecs, Spanish colonisation attempted to destroy Andean religion and culture. However, the Andean people continued to resist by blending their beliefs and traditions with Catholicism. For example, Pachamama was identified with the Virgin Mary and Inti was identified with Jesus. Indigenous dances and offerings continue to this day as part of South American Christian practices.

Check your understanding

1. What did Pizarro think was in South America?

2. Why was the Inca state weakened by Pizarro's arrival in 1532?

3. What happened after Friar Vicente de Valverde's speech to Atahualpa?

4. How did Manco II rebel against the Spanish from 1536?

5. What was the most significant reason for the defeat of the Inca?

Knowledge organiser

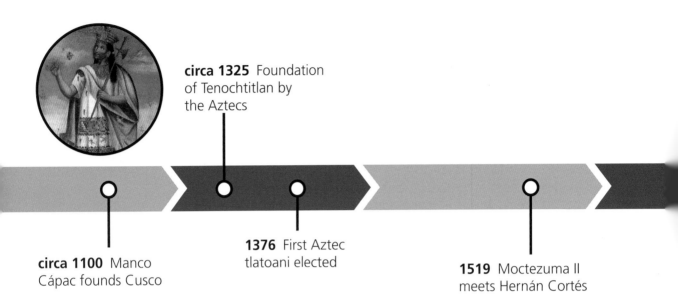

circa 1325 Foundation of Tenochtitlan by the Aztecs

circa 1100 Manco Cápac founds Cusco

1376 First Aztec tlatoani elected

1519 Moctezuma II meets Hernán Cortés

Key vocabulary

Aclla Cuna Girls from age 8 who were taken from each province and kept secluded while performing religious duties

Amautas Teachers in the Inca empire known as 'wise ones'

Andean People and culture relating to the Andes mountains in South America

Aztecs Civilisation that ruled Mesoamerica in the 14th to 16th centuries

Chalchiuatl Mesoamerican term for blood, meaning 'precious liquid'

Capacocha Incan child sacrifice ritual that established Incan control over villages

Chicha Beer made from maize

Chinampas 'Floating gardens' developed by the Aztecs in Tenochtitlan to farm crops

Coca Plant in South America which is the source of the drug cocaine

Conquistadors Spanish and Portuguese soldiers that conquered the Americas

Coricancha Golden enclosure in Cusco with important temples to Inti and Mama Killa, and where the royal mummies were preserved

Cusco Capital of the Inca empire

Huacas Sacred Inca sites such as springs, mountains and caves

Inca *(also spelled Inka)* Civilisation that ruled South America in the 12th–16th centuries

Lake Texcoco Lake in Mexico, centre of the Aztec empire

Lake Titicaca Important lake for the Inca empire in Peru

Maize Sweetcorn, a native Mesoamerican plant

Maya Civilisation of city states that existed from the 4th century in the jungle terrain of the Yucatan peninsula in Mexico

Mesoamerica Region of modern Mexico, Belize, Guatemala and Honduras

Mit'a Compulsory public service for men aged 15–50 in the Inca empire

Nahuatl Language of Mesoamerica and the Aztecs

Obsidian Volcanic glass used as a sharp cutting tool

Polygamy The practice of having more than one wife at the same time

Popol Vuh Ancient Maya mythological narrative, first written down in the 16th century

Enquiry Question: What contributed most significantly to the Spanish colonisation of the Aztec and Inca empires?

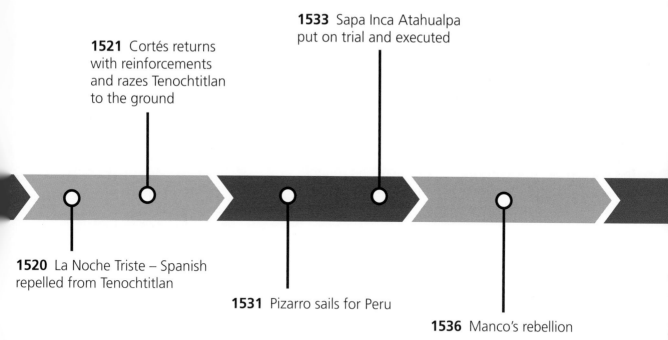

1521 Cortés returns with reinforcements and razes Tenochtitlan to the ground

1533 Sapa Inca Atahualpa put on trial and executed

1520 La Noche Triste – Spanish repelled from Tenochtitlan

1531 Pizarro sails for Peru

1536 Manco's rebellion

Key vocabulary

Quauhpilli Eagle Noble warriors in Aztec society who had achieved more than 20 acts of bravery

Quipu Knots that could be 'read' to record events in Inca society

Shaman Priest believed to have access to the spirit world through the consumption of hallucinogenic drugs

Tenochtitlan Capital of the Aztec empire in Mexico, famous for its grand size

Tlatoani Title for the ruler of the Aztecs, which means 'speaker' in Nahuatl

Tlaxcala Enemy state of the Aztecs who were forced to compete in the Flower Wars

Tribute Payment paid by one state to another as a sign of respect and dependence

Tzompantli Skull racks in Aztec cities to remember those who had been sacrificed

Ullamalitztli Mesoamerican ball game played with a 4-kg rubber ball bounced from the hips, elbows and knees

Vilcabamba Centre of the Neo-Inca state from 1536 to 1572, high in the Andes mountains

Key people

Atahualpa Sapa Inca when Pizarro arrived

Diego de Almagro Ally and eventual enemy of Pizarro

Diego Velázquez Governor of Cuba

Francisco Pizarro Conquistador of Peru

Friar Vicente de Valverde Priest who tried to convert Atahualpa to Christianity

Hernán Cortés Conquistador of Mexico

Huascar Brother of Atahualpa who was killed in civil war

Malintzin Enslaved woman given to Cortés who became crucial for interpreting the Nahuatl language

Manco Cápac First ruler of the Inca

Manco II Led Inca rebellion in 1536

Moctezuma II Aztec tlatoani when Cortés arrived

Unit 8: The Ottoman Empire
Rise of the Ottomans

During the early 14th century, a Turkish Muslim warlord began conquering much of Asia Minor. His name was Osman, and he would become the founder of the Ottoman Empire.

Legend has it that **Osman** once had a dream that a tree sprouted from his navel and its shade encompassed the world. This inspired him to expand the territory under his control, taking advantage of the weakening Christian **Byzantine** empire, his fiercest rival.

In 1301 Osman had his first victory against the Byzantines. Under his successors, the **Ottomans** (as they became known) managed to conquer almost all the Byzantine empire's remaining territories, including Greece, Bulgaria, Romania and Serbia. However, despite being surrounded on all fronts, the strategically important city of **Constantinople** remained in Byzantine hands.

Map of Christian Constantinople by Anselmo Banduri 1711

The conquest of Constantinople

Since the city's foundation by the Roman emperor Constantine in 324 CE, no army had successfully breached the famous layers of defensive walls that surrounded Constantinople. Positioned in the narrow straits between the Black Sea and the Mediterranean, Constantinople's sheltered harbour was a global trading hub. The Byzantines protected the harbour with a huge chain that was raised when enemy ships approached. The city was also full of famous art and architecture. Its cathedral **Hagia Sophia**, built in 537 CE, was the world's largest domed church for almost 1000 years.

Some of the Byzantine defensive walls of Constantinople (modern-day Istanbul, in Turkey)

In 1451 Mehmed II became the Ottoman **sultan** aged just 19. Following a hadith (saying) of the Prophet Muhammed that stated 'verily you shall conquer Constantinople', more than 12 Muslim armies had tried to break into Constantinople over the previous 900 years – but without success. However, Mehmed was determined to conquer the city.

Mehmed spared no expense in trying to find a way to break into Constantinople. He started by building a castle to the north of the city, to cut supply lines to the Byzantines. He also enlarged the Ottoman navy to block the entrance from the Mediterranean and mustered up 160 000 troops for the siege. He even hired a Hungarian engineer named **Orban** to build the largest cannon the world had ever seen, known as 'Basilica'. It took a team of 60 oxen to haul Orban's 9-metre-long cannon towards Constantinople, so it could fire cannonballs weighing 500 kg to bombard the city walls.

The Byzantine emperor **Constantine XI** knew that he was in a perilous position. Due to the shrinking Byzantine Empire, Constantinople was a city in decline with only 10 per cent of its former population. Some areas of the city were even being used as farmland. Surrounded by Ottoman territory and almost bankrupt, Constantine had to rely on just 10 000 troops, led by an Italian mercenary named **Giovanni Giustiniani Longo**, to defend the city. Just as during the Crusades, the Byzantine emperor appealed to Western Europe for help and waited nervously, hoping for a response.

Despite being severely outnumbered and facing heavy cannon bombardment day and night, Giustiniani was an able commander. As the weeks wore on, Mehmed became increasingly frustrated that his army had still not managed to breach the walls. His navy had also failed to stop supply ships reaching Constantinople, and the sultan feared growing rumours of rebellion in his army.

Mehmed then came up with a plan. If he could attack the walls of the city that faced the water, then Giustiniani's limited troops would be further stretched to defend all nine miles of walls. Mehmed could not get his ships past the defensive chain in the water, so he planned to move his ships overland, rolling them over greased logs and continuously firing cannonballs to hide the sound of falling trees. On the morning of 23 April 1453, the Byzantines awoke to see the astonishing sight of the Ottoman navy sitting in their own harbour.

Bad omens such as thunderstorms and an eclipse broke the spirit of the Byzantines, who feared God had abandoned them. On 29 May, Mehmed finally breached the walls of Constantinople, and wave after wave of attackers stormed the city. Constantine XI was offered an escape route, but instead charged towards the fighting and his own death.

After a 53-day siege, Mehmed II had broken into the fortified city that had foiled so many conquerors before him, succeeding in his ambition to extinguish the Byzantine Empire once and for all. He was only 21 years old.

Fact

The Byzantines had used flammable substances to set fire to enemy ships since the 7th century. When Mehmed used Serbian miners to dig underneath the walls of Constantinople and 'undermine' their foundations, a Scottish mercenary named John Grant counter-mined, igniting and then pouring a liquid known as 'Greek fire' onto the miners and saving the walls.

Turkish Ottoman Sultan Mehmed II the Conqueror (1432–81)

Ancient role models

Mehmed II spoke at least six languages and saw himself as the inheritor of the ancient Greek and Roman civilisations. Mehmed added 'Kayser-I Rum' (Caesar of Rome) to the official titles of the Ottoman sultan, and Constantinople became the new capital of the Ottoman Empire. He kept the Greco-Roman architecture of the city intact, converting churches into mosques and rebuilding the battered city as a symbol of Islamic greatness.

Check your understanding

1. What did Osman's dream inspire?
2. Why did the Ottomans want the city of Constantinople?
3. How did Mehmed II prepare for the siege of Constantinople?
4. How did Mehmed II finally breach the walls and conquer Constantinople?
5. Did Constantine XI have realistic hopes of victory against Mehmed II?

Unit 8: The Ottoman Empire
Suleiman 'the Magnificent'

The conquest of Constantinople marked a shift in power as the Ottomans became Europe's largest and most dominant empire.

The great conqueror Mehmed II did not stop at Constantinople but expanded the Ottoman Empire further into Greece, Serbia, Bosnia and Albania. He even briefly captured the city of Otranto, in south-east Italy, in 1480 CE. During the reign of his grandson **Selim I**, the empire grew by another 70 per cent. Selim conquered Egypt and the Middle East, bringing the pilgrimage routes to Mecca and Medina under Ottoman control. The Barbary coastal states of North Africa (Morocco, Algeria, Tunisia and Libya) also became part of this ever-expanding empire.

Selim's son, **Suleiman I**, ruled from 1520 to 1566. During his reign, the Ottoman Empire reached its greatest extent at 2.3 million square kilometres. Suleiman pressed further into central Europe and threatened the Habsburg monarchy of the **Holy Roman Empire**. He led the Ottoman victory at the Battle of Mohács in 1526, where 18 000 Hungarians died, including King Louis II of Hungary (compared to the loss of only 2000 Ottomans).

Suleiman 'the Magnificent', painted around 1530

Having conquered Hungary, Suleiman then laid siege to Vienna with an army of 100 000 troops in 1529. Suleiman was met with defeat after running out of supplies and the oncoming of winter, but it was the start of 150 years of conflict between the Habsburgs and the Ottomans. The strain of this conflict would prevent the Holy Roman Emperors from effectively crushing the emerging Protestant reformation.

European treaties

Aside from waging war against European monarchs, Suleiman was also an influential statesman, exploiting the divisions between Catholic kings and the new rising Protestant movement. Western Europeans called him 'Suleiman the Magnificent' and he was seen as a hugely powerful ruler, looked at with awe for the far reaches of his empire, the great victories he achieved and the huge wealth he amassed. The elites of Europe sought trade deals and military alliances with him, as well as emulating his clothing style with silks bought from the Ottoman Empire.

In 1536, Suleiman and Francis I of France agreed the Franco–Ottoman alliance against the Holy Roman Empire and the Papal States. This was a mutually beneficial agreement, as the Holy Roman emperor was a key rival against both monarchs. Henry VIII of England considered joining the alliance after breaking from the Roman Catholic Church as a way to weaken the power of the Holy Roman Emperor Charles V and the Pope. French ambassadors even came to London to broker a deal, but it was never concluded. Nevertheless, in 1553 Suleiman met the Englishman

Portuguese clashes

In the 16th century, the Portuguese had begun establishing trading posts in the Indian Ocean. From Somalia to Indonesia, Ottoman ships were engaged in naval campaigns to remove Portuguese influence. Surviving letters between Suleiman and the Mughal emperor Akbar the Great show the extent of diplomatic relations between distant countries.

Anthony Jenkinson in Aleppo, Syria, and granted him the right to trade in cloth and silk in Ottoman lands.

Suleiman 'the lawgiver'

The Ottomans referred to Suleiman as 'Kanuni' ('lawgiver') for the way he revised and developed the Kanun imperial law codes, first written by Mehmed II. The Kanun laws were derived from the Sultan himself and were therefore seen as separate from Sharia religious law, which derived from the Quran. This allowed Suleiman to have more personal control over criminal laws, taxation and landholding.

Significantly, many of these laws protected the religious minorities who lived within the Ottoman Empire such as Jews and Christians. These religious minorities were allowed to set up independent communities called **millets**. Millets could follow their own customs and have their own courts of law for cases not involving Muslims. Their communities governed themselves with little involvement from the Ottomans, in exchange for loyalty to the Sultan and the payment of special taxes. This granted religious minorities a larger degree of autonomy and toleration than in the rest of Europe and made Ottoman cities famously cosmopolitan and multicultural.

The Suleimaniye Mosque in Istanbul, built between 1550 and 1558 CE

Art and architecture

Suleiman was a patron of the arts, who funded artistic societies known as **Ehl-i-Hiref** ('Groups of the Talented'). This encouraged artists and craftsmen to develop a distinctive Ottoman style. Beautiful painted manuscripts depicting court life were produced and Suleiman himself wrote some of the most celebrated Ottoman poems.

Suleiman appointed Mimar Sinan as the Chief Royal Architect to create magnificent Ottoman buildings such as the Suleimaniye mosque, completed in 1557, which remained the largest in Constantinople for 462 years. This style of mosque complex spread to all reaches of the Ottoman Empire, and typically included a hospital, **hamam**, school, library, **caravanserai** and a kitchen to serve food to the poor. Blue and white Iznik tiles inspired by Chinese porcelain designs were common decoration in such buildings.

Fact

Near the end of his reign, Suleiman was told that his two favourite sons, Mustafa and Bayezid, were conspiring against him and he was forced to have them both executed. He was wracked with guilt for this decision and retreated into **Topkapi Palace**, leaving the **Grand Vizier** to rule on his behalf.

Check your understanding

1. Which countries had the Ottoman Empire expanded into when Suleiman I became sultan in 1520?
2. Which monarchy was a bitter enemy of Suleiman I?
3. Which European countries had peaceful interactions with Suleiman?
4. How did Suleiman influence society, art and architecture in the Ottoman Empire?
5. What was the most significant impact of Suleiman I's reign?

Clashes with Safavid Persia

While Europe worried about Ottoman expansion in the west, a new empire threatened Ottoman control in the east.

One of the biggest divisions in the Islamic faith is between the **Sunni** and **Shia** branches, or orders. While they share many of the same beliefs and practices, there are differences in rituals, laws and organisation. These differences trace back to a disagreement over who should have succeeded the Prophet Muhammed after his death in 632 CE.

The Ottomans were of the Sunni order. They stressed the importance of the Prophet Muhammed's words but believed that subsequent leaders need not be direct descendants of the Prophet. The Shia order believed that the Prophet Muhammed's divine guidance was passed down to 12 of his descendants, the last of whom disappeared in 878 CE. They believed this '12th imam' would return to restore justice to Earth.

Around 1500, a 12-year-old boy from Iran named **Ismail** claimed to be the representative of the '12th imam'. He quickly gained a devoted following among the Shia order, and his armies took control of Iran, Azerbaijan and Iraq, lands that once made up the ancient Persian Empire. Ismail declared himself **shah**, the historic title of the Persian kings, and began the **Safavid** dynasty, proclaiming the Shia faith as the official religion of his lands.

Abbas I the Great, Shah of the Safavid dynasty from 1588 to 1629

Ottoman–Safavid wars

The territorial gains the Safavids made, as well as their ability to convert many people to the Shia order, threatened the power of the Ottoman Empire. This led to centuries of rivalry between the two empires. The Ottoman sultan Selim I declared the Shia were heretics in order to legitimise attacking fellow Muslims. In 1514, Selim I crushed Ismail I's forces at the Battle of Chaldiran, weakening Ismail's claims of invincibility.

Under the next three Safavid shahs, civil wars and power struggles broke out, which the Ottomans exploited; for example, Suleiman I captured Baghdad and most of Iraq in 1534. It wasn't until the accession of **Shah Abbas I** in 1587 that the Safavids began to expand their empire again.

During his 42-year reign, Shah Abbas reorganised the military with a standing army, artillery (canons) and muskets (rifles). He actively sought diplomatic links with other countries, seeking European help against the Ottomans and expanding his territory when the Ottomans were distracted in the west. As the Ottomans represented Sunni Islam, Shah Abbas often treated Sunnis living in Safavid territory harshly. However, he was more tolerant towards Christians to show his potential European allies that the Ottomans were their common enemy.

Tudor support for Ottoman attacks

Elizabeth I wrote letters throughout her reign to the Ottoman sultan Murad III to increase diplomatic ties. From these letters, we know that the Tudors sent metal stripped from Catholic churches and sold it to the Ottomans so they could make more weaponry in their wars against Spain and the Safavids. This benefitted England, who was also at war with Spain at this time (see Unit 2, Chapter 4).

Life in Isfahan

Shah Abbas I built **Isfahan** in central Iran as an imperial capital to rival Constantinople. It was luxuriously decorated with monumental buildings and attracted a cosmopolitan society. With 163 mosques, 250 hamams and 1800 shops, Isfahan contained some of the best Islamic architecture in the world. Isfahan's many impressive buildings included the Si-o-se-pol ('Bridge of 33 arches'), which spans the Zayandeh River. Underground channels brought water to the city, which overflowed with baths and fountains. The Shah Mosque was decorated in striking turquoise and mirrored tiles, which created a dazzling effect in the Iranian sun.

Shah Mosque in Isfahan, in modern-day Iran. Also known as Imam Mosque, its construction was completed in 1629

At the **Naqsh-e Jahan Square**, a huge stretch of land bounded by arches served as the space for a **bazaar** and coffee houses. Foreign merchants would gather in **Isfahan**, which was a vital stopping point on the Silk Road, to sell their goods. This also enabled the distribution of Persian works of art such as silks, velvets, carpets and painted manuscripts, which elites across the world enjoyed

Naqsh-e Jahan Square in Isfahan, in modern-day Iran

collecting. The most famous manuscript was an epic poem called the **Shahnameh** that the Safavid shahs promoted as a defence of their right to rule as inheritors of the ancient history of Persia. More than 70 000 copies were produced, and single sheets of popular scenes were also sold separately for collectors.

At the Chehel Sotoun ('Forty Pillar Palace') the Shah held royal feasts where hundreds of people were invited. These were based on the ancient feasting rituals of Persian kings taken from the Shahnameh. This was a more open, ceremonial and public type of kingship compared to the secretive seclusion of the Ottoman sultan and Mughal emperors (see Chapter 5, this unit).

Fact

Some historians have labelled the Ottoman, Safavid and Mughal empires as the Islamic 'gunpowder empires'. They were viewed in awe by Western Europe for their mastery of firearms, and also for their strong military forces, their expanding economies, patronage of the arts and centralised control.

Check your understanding

1. What is the difference between the Sunni and Shia orders of Islam?
2. What did Ismail I do?
3. Why did the Ottomans and Safavids clash?
4. What did Shah Abbas I do to improve the Safavid Empire?
5. Why was the rise of the Safavid Empire significant?

Unit 8: The Ottoman Empire
Ottoman–Venetian wars

The Ottomans and Venetians fought for control of the Mediterranean over a period of more than 200 years, which included seven separate wars.

Since the Middle Ages, the Republic of Venice had been one of the Mediterranean's leading powers, making favourable trade deals with a variety of countries, and colonising strategic ports across the Mediterranean. Venetians became prime importers of goods from the East and this trade **monopoly** made Venice the wealthiest city in Europe.

With the growth of the Ottoman Empire, Venice needed to negotiate its position with this new power. At times the relationship was peaceful, but they were ultimately rivals for dominance of the Mediterranean. There were seven Ottoman–Venetian wars between 1463 and 1718, during which the Ottomans captured practically all of the Venetian colonies, establishing themselves – along with the **Barbary corsairs** – as the rulers of the Mediterranean seas.

Barbary corsairs

The Barbary states (Morocco, Algeria, Tunisia and Libya) were brought under Ottoman control by Oruch and Khizir Reis, known as the 'Barbarossa' brothers ('Barbarossa' means 'redbeard' in Italian). While the Barbary corsairs were officially part of the Ottoman Empire and provided important harbours for the Ottoman navy, they mostly operated independently of the Ottoman Sultan, to make money for themselves. For this reason, the meaning of the word 'corsair' is similar to 'pirate'.

The Barbary corsairs were greatly feared. They roamed the Mediterranean, interrupting trade routes and attacking coastal towns to capture people to enslave. It is estimated that up to 1.25 million people were enslaved through Barbary raids, which extended from Italy and Spain to sometimes as far afield as West Africa, England, Ireland and even Iceland.

The Battle of Lepanto, 1571

The Fourth Ottoman–Venetian war started when the Ottomans invaded the Venetian colony of Cyprus in 1570. Since the conquest of Constantinople in 1453, the Christian countries of Western Europe had failed to unite against the Ottomans. However, in this conflict, Pope Pius V helped to create a '**Holy League**' made up of Spain, Venice and other Italian city states.

On 7 October 1571, the Holy League fleet of around 210 ships, led by King Philip II of Spain's half-brother Don John of Austria, met the Ottomans at Lepanto on the western coast of Greece. While the Ottomans had more ships, they were all galley-style ships, relying on oarsmen ramming into other vessels. However, the Venetians had six galleasses, with sails as well as oars and mounted with cannons. With this firepower at their disposal, more than 117 Ottoman boats were captured and 50 sunk, while the Holy League lost only 15.

ARUCH en CHERIDYN BARBAROSSA

Dutch engraving of the Turkish corsairs Oruch and Khizir Barbarossa, who lived from the late 15th to mid 16th centuries

In Western Europe, the Holy League's victory at Lepanto was seen as a huge breakthrough against the seemingly invincible and ever-expanding Ottoman Empire. European printing presses circulated news of the victory with speed, and the victory served great symbolic importance during a period when Europe was torn by the Wars of Religion (see Unit 6, Chapter 4). However, the Holy League quickly disintegrated, and the Ottomans built a new fleet within a year. The Holy League also failed to reclaim any land from the Ottoman Empire – not even the island of Cyprus.

The Battle of Lepanto, 1571, when the Holy League inflicted a major defeat on the fleet of the Ottoman Empire

When asked about the defeat at Lepanto by the Venetian ambassador, the Ottoman Grand Vizier Sokullu Mehmed Pasha responded: "When we took Cyprus, we cut off one of your arms. You defeated our fleet, which meant nothing more than shaving our beard. A missing arm cannot be replaced but a shaved beard grows thicker."

The Great Turkish War, 1683–99

The sixth Ottoman–Venetian war became known as 'The Great Turkish War' for the 15 years of bitter struggles it provoked. The Christian powers of Europe managed to come together in another 'Holy League', which for the first time included Russia. In 1683, the Ottomans attempted a second siege of Vienna with 150 000 soldiers. Vienna had been weakened by a recent outbreak of plague, but the Ottoman plans were thwarted by a Christian relief army of 60 000 appearing over the hills. The fast cavalry charge of 3000 Winged Hussars led by the Polish king John Sobieski broke the unprepared Ottoman lines and caused them to flee.

Contemporary engraving of the destruction of the Parthenon in Athens, Greece, in 1687 by the explosion of the Turks' gunpowder stores

The Treaty of Karlowitz in 1699 ended the Great Turkish War, transferring areas of modern-day Hungary, Croatia and Ukraine to the Habsburg monarchy. This was the first significant loss of territory for the Ottomans since the expansion of their empire 200 years previously.

Venetian vandalism

During the Great Turkish War, Venetian captain Francesco Morosini had orders to recapture southern Greece and seize Athens from the Ottomans. The city's famous Acropolis was being used as a gunpowder store by the Ottomans, who presumed that the Venetians wouldn't attack the ancient temples. However, on 26 September 1687, Morosini fired his cannons and the Parthenon exploded, giving it the distinctive ruined shape it has to this day.

Check your understanding

1. How did the Republic of Venice become wealthy?

2. What were the Venetians and Ottomans fighting for control over?

3. Why did the Ottomans lose the Battle of Lepanto in 1571?

4. Why was the Battle of Lepanto not a huge loss for the Ottomans?

5. Why was the Great Turkish War significant?

Unit 8: The Ottoman Empire
Ottoman society

The Ottoman Empire managed to maintain a multi-ethnic and multi-religious society for centuries. It depended upon an unusual system of slavery to function.

One of the biggest problems within European courts was the rivalry of hereditary aristocrats with the monarch. These aristocrats aimed to marry into royalty or hold important positions of power, often sparking rebellions. The Ottomans avoided this problem by creating an aristocracy of peoples of enslaved origin. Almost all the key positions of power were held by enslaved people who, as the sultan's personal possessions, were loyal to him alone. For example, every sultan's mother was enslaved and almost all his Grand Viziers had been enslaved during their lifetime.

One important group of enslaved people who saw social advancement in the empire were the **janissaries**. These elite troops were the first modern standing army in Europe and were greatly feared for both their military discipline and extensive use of firearms. They were captured and enslaved as children via the **devshirme** system. This involved rounding up boys from Christian families in the Balkans and bringing them to Constantinople, where they were converted to Islam. They were forbidden to marry before the age of 40 and owed their complete allegiance to the sultan, serving as his bodyguard. They wore distinctive uniforms and were paid generous salaries. Their proximity to the sultan gave them important political power and they became part of the ruling class of the Ottoman Empire.

Life in Topkapi Palace

Topkapi Palace was a symbol of the imperial magnificence of the Ottoman sultans, with colourfully tiled buildings, fountains, gardens and exotic animals. Aside from being the sultan's main residence, it was also the centre of governance – where the imperial treasury, royal mint and **Diwan** (imperial council) were located. While the sultan did not attend every meeting of the Diwan, a window with a golden grill allowed him to watch over the proceedings unobserved. This meant he could check whether his ministers and Grand Vizier were being truthful when they had separate audiences with him.

The Topkapi Palace also had religious significance by safeguarding holy relics of Islam such as the cloak and tooth of Muhammed. An aura of holy silence was maintained around the sultan. He appointed deaf mutes to be his closest companions and converse in sign language. The sultan also employed dwarves as servants, so that he appeared larger and more powerful than those around him.

The **harem** was the living quarters for the sultan's mother, wife, daughters and other female relatives as well as young sons. It was here that future

> ### Fact
> From 1451 to 1603, new sultans would kill all their brothers when they ascended the throne. Mehmed II introduced royal fratricide as a way to avoid civil war. In 1595, Mehmed III killed 19 of his brothers to secure his throne. The sight of so many coffins leaving Topkapi Palace caused outrage and led to the end of the practice.

Janissaries to Suleiman I; detail from a Turkish illustrated manuscript

sultans would be educated and where many high officials of the Ottoman state sought a wife. Members of the harem came from all over the empire and were treated as the sultan's personal possessions; they were not allowed to leave Topkapi Palace without his permission. Some women were also enslaved here and kept as potential concubines for the sultan. At its height, the harem in Topkapi Palace housed over 300 women, some of whom never even saw the sultan during their lifetime in the maze-like corridors of the palace.

Topkapi Palace in Istanbul. Its construction began in 1459 under Mehmed II

To ensure that the 'modesty' of the women in the harem was kept secure, only **eunuchs** were allowed to guard this section of the palace. The most important eunuch was the **Kizlar Agha**, who was the fourth highest ranking official in the Ottoman state. Over time, the Kizlar Agha played a huge role in the downfall of various sultans and Grand Viziers, particularly during the period of the Sultanate of Women.

The importance of Topkapi Palace increased during the 17th century, when a succession of young, incompetent and mentally ill sultans came to power. This resulted in the sultan becoming increasingly secluded from the rest of the world while the Diwan, Grand Vizier, janissaries, chief eunuchs and women of the harem all vied for power.

Hurrem Sultan, who rose from being an enslaved **concubine** in Suleiman I's harem to become his legal wife and Empress consort

The Sultanate of Women, 1533–1656

From 1533 to 1656, the wives and mothers of sultans, despite being enslaved concubines, managed to wield significant influence over Ottoman court life, much to the disdain of the Grand Vizier and janissaries.

Two of the most significant women in this period were Hurrem Sultan and Kosem Sultan. Surviving letters during Suleiman I's reign show that Hurrem wrote to international monarchs on foreign policy and approved finances for new buildings in several cities, including a large hamam complex in Constantinople. Kosem was the mother of two sultans and the grandmother of another. She wielded significant influence within Topkapi Palace for decades, even ruling as regent of the empire in her own right from 1623 to 1632 when Murad IV became sultan at age 11.

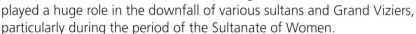

Kosem Sultan

Check your understanding

1. Why were the janissaries feared?

2. What was the devshirme?

3. What important buildings were inside Topkapi Palace?

4. What was the purpose of eunuchs in Topkapi Palace?

5. Did enslaved people hold the most influence in the Ottoman court?

Unit 8: The Ottoman Empire
Knowledge organiser

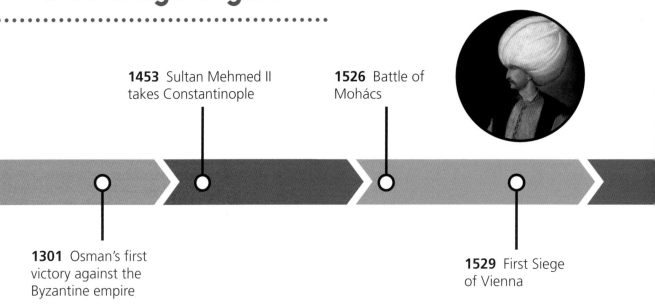

1301 Osman's first victory against the Byzantine empire

1453 Sultan Mehmed II takes Constantinople

1526 Battle of Mohács

1529 First Siege of Vienna

Key vocabulary

Barbary corsairs Pirates based along the Barbary coast of North Africa

Bazaar Covered marketplace, associated with the Islamic world

Byzantine Associated with Byzantium, the Greek-speaking offshoot of the Roman Empire with Constantinople as its capital city

Caravanserai An inn with a central courtyard for merchants on a trade route

Concubine A person, usually enslaved, and used for sex

Constantinople Capital of the Ottoman Empire from 1453

Devshirme System of removing young boys from their Christian families to serve the sultan

Diwan Imperial council for the Ottoman sultan

Ehl-i-Hiref 'Groups of the Talented' – artistic societies funded by Suleiman I, which developed a distinctive Ottoman style of art, architecture and poetry

Eunuch A man who has been castrated (had his genitals removed)

Grand Vizier Special advisor to the Ottoman sultan, and head of the imperial government

Hagia Sophia Enormous Byzantine cathedral in Constantinople, converted into a mosque by Mehmed II

Hamam Public bath associated with the Islamic world

Harem Domestic space in a Muslim household reserved for women

Holy League Alliance of Christian European states against the Ottomans during the Ottoman–Venetian wars

Holy Roman Empire Empire during the medieval and Early Modern periods that covered modern-day Germany, Austria, Switzerland and parts of Italy and the Netherlands

Isfahan New capital of the Safavid empire under Shah Abbas I

Janissaries Elite troops recruited from Christian families, who converted to Islam and were loyal to the sultan

Kizlar Agha Chief Eunuch of the Ottoman Sultan's harem

Monopoly Exclusive possession of a certain trade, so ensuring no competition

Millet Recognised religious or ethnic group in the Ottoman Empire

Naqsh-e Jahan Square Monumental marketplace and garden built by Shah Abbas I

Enquiry question: How serious a threat to Europe was the Ottoman Empire?

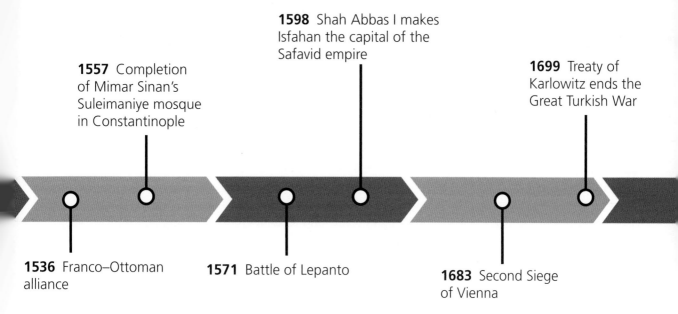

1598 Shah Abbas I makes Isfahan the capital of the Safavid empire

1557 Completion of Mimar Sinan's Suleimaniye mosque in Constantinople

1699 Treaty of Karlowitz ends the Great Turkish War

1536 Franco–Ottoman alliance

1571 Battle of Lepanto

1683 Second Siege of Vienna

Key vocabulary

Ottoman Empire based in Turkey that controlled parts of Europe, Africa and the Middle East from the 14th to the 20th centuries

Safavid Ruling dynasty of Persia, 1501–1736

Shah Title for the ruler of Persia under the Safavid empire

Shahnameh Epic poem on painted manuscripts promoted by the Safavid shahs to show their inheritance of ancient Persia

Shia Order of Islam followed by the Safavids

Sultan Ruler of a large Islamic state, such as the Ottoman Empire

Sunni Order of Islam followed by the Ottomans

Topkapi Palace Royal residence and administrative centre in Constantinople

Key people

Constantine XI Last emperor of the Byzantine emperor, who reigned from 1449 to 1453

Giovanni Giustiniani Longo Italian mercenary who commanded the defence of Constantinople in 1453

Hurrem Sultan First wife of Suleiman I, who held diplomatic power and financed great building projects

Ismail Founder of the Safavid empire in 1501

John Sobieski King of Poland who led the Winged Hussars cavalry charge to break the Ottoman second siege of Vienna in 1683

Kosem Sultan Powerful mother of two sultans, who ruled the Ottoman Empire as regent from 1623 to 1632

Mehmed II the Conqueror Ottoman sultan who conquered Constantinople in 1453

Mehmed III Sultan (1595–1603), who killed 19 brothers when he gained the throne

Osman 14th-century founder of the Ottoman dynasty

Selim I Ottoman sultan (1512–20), who conquered Egypt and won the first victory against the Safavids in 1514

Shah Abbas I Safavid ruler (1587–1629), who was highly esteemed and founded Isfahan as the new capital city

Suleiman I Ottoman sultan (1520–66), who expanded the empire to its largest extent in the 16th century; he was known as 'Suleiman the Magnificent' in the West

Babur of Kabul

In the early 16th century, a Muslim warlord from central Asia conquered much of northern India. He became the founder of a dynasty called the **Mughals**, who would rule India for centuries.

This ruler was Babur of **Kabul**. He was born in 1483 in the **Ferghana Valley**, in what is today Uzbekistan in central Asia. At birth he was called Zahir-ud-din Muhammad, but he later took the name Babur, which means 'tiger'. Babur was descended on his father's side from Timur Lenk and on his mother's from Chinggis Khan – the two greatest Mongol conquerors.

Babur was famous for his strength and skill as a warrior. He commanded armies from a very young age, conquering the great city of Samarkand when he was only 14 – although he lost control of it shortly afterwards. It was said that he could run up slopes carrying a man on his back, and that he had swum across every river he ever encountered, including the Ganges. He was ruthless to his enemies, but he was also a sensitive and intellectual man who loved gardening and poetry, and wrote many books. During his conquest of India, he personally wrote detailed reports on the country's culture, wildlife and flowers.

> **Fact**
>
> Babur thought of himself as Turkic (the native people of his region), and always referred to himself and his followers as Turks. However, he and his heirs were often identified by others as Mongol rulers. The name 'Mughal' is simply the Persian version of the word 'Mongol'.

The conquest of India

Babur became ruler of Ferghana at the age of 11, but he was soon forced out of his homeland by the rise of a powerful Uzbek warlord named Muhammad Shaybani Khan, who defeated him in battle in 1501. Babur became a wandering prince, seeking an empire to rule. The place he really wanted to rule was Samarkand, which had been the capital of his ancestor Timur. However, after failing again to capture it, he turned south and took control of the city of Kabul in Afghanistan in 1504.

Babur spent 15 years consolidating his rule of Afghanistan, and failed in several more attempts to conquer central Asia. In 1519 he gave up on Samarkand, and instead turned his attention south-east – towards India. India at the time was fragmented into many small kingdoms. Most of the states in the north were either small Hindu kingdoms called the **Rajput states**, or they were **sultanates** under Islamic rulers. India's most powerful rulers were the Lodi, an Afghan dynasty who governed much of northern India, including the sultanate of **Delhi**.

Babur holding Court, 1589

Babur originally planned only to conquer the **Punjab**, India's north-western region. However, he was soon tempted to go further. In 1526 Babur defeated Ibrahim, the sultan of Delhi, at the Battle of Panipat. Here, Babur proved his skill as a general by beating an army that was said to be 100 000 soldiers (and many war elephants) with a force of only 12 000 men. Babur went on to seize Delhi, then conquered many of the Rajput states over the years that followed. He created an empire that stretched from Kabul in Afghanistan across most of northern India.

Humayun

In 1530, Babur's eldest son, Humayun, fell very sick. Babur is said to have prayed by his son's bedside for his own life to be taken instead. Humayun recovered – but Babur sickened and died. He was buried back in Kabul.

Humayun struggled to hold his father's empire together. His four brothers all felt that kingship should be shared between them all, so they carved out their own kingdoms and refused to support him. Soon Humayun was driven from Delhi by Sher Shah (often known as Sher Khan), an Afghan warlord based in eastern India. After losing the Battle of Kanauj in 1540, Humayun fled India and was given shelter in the court of Shah Tahmasp I, ruler of the **Safavid empire** in Persia. Sher Shah was left to rule what had been Babur's Indian empire.

It was only ten years after Sher Shah's death that Humayun dared to reclaim India. In 1555, with the help of Persian troops, he successfully returned and reconquered part of his father's empire. Yet less than a year later in January 1556, he died by falling down a staircase in his library. Humayun's son Akbar succeeded him aged only 13.

Fact

Babur was not impressed with India. He wrote that it had "no good horses, no good dogs, no grapes, musk-melons or first-rate fruits, no ice or cold water, no good bread or cooked food in the bazaars, no hot baths, no colleges, no candles, no torches, and no candlesticks."

Check your understanding

1. Why were Babur and the emperors of India who followed him known as Mughals?

2. How did the teenage Babur become a 'wandering prince'?

3. How was Babur able to win the Battle of Panipat?

4. How was the Safavid Persian empire responsible for Babur's dynasty continuing to rule India?

5. Why was Babur not fully enthusiastic about becoming ruler of northern India?

Unit 9: Mughal India
Akbar the Great

Akbar – the third Mughal emperor – is often said to have been the greatest ruler in Indian history. It was he who truly made the Mughal empire one of the most formidable powers of the Early Modern world.

Akbar was brave and intelligent, but reckless and headstrong. He preferred sports to study, and he remained almost illiterate throughout his life – many scholars think he suffered from dyslexia. He loved hunting, shooting and riding his fighting elephants, and he once killed a tiger with only a sword. Yet he also appreciated the arts: he collected beautiful books and paid for a department of court painters who produced many great works of art. Akbar also took an unusual interest in the common people of India. It was said that he sometimes slipped out of his palace and mingled with them, dressed in ordinary clothes so that none of them knew who he was.

The emperor Akbar with his cavalry; detail from a Moghul painting, circa 1590

Akbar's reign

During the first few years of Akbar's reign, when he ruled only a small area of northern India, his kingdom was effectively in the hands of **regents**. They did much to reconquer parts of India that Babur had ruled, including the Punjab. However, when Akbar took control himself in 1562, aged 19, there was still much of his grandfather's empire left to reconquer.

Akbar set about this task with determination. First, he married the daughter of the greatest of the Rajput lords, the **Raja** (king) of Amber, who had been the first of the princes in western India to accept Mughal authority. The Raja was allowed to keep running his own lands, so long as he gave loyalty to Akbar. This proved an effective arrangement, and Akbar extended it across his empire, allowing defeated enemies to keep their local power so long as they gave him their loyalty. He went on to unify all northern India, including the far northern region of Kashmir and far eastern region of Bengal. By the time of his death, Akbar ruled a massive band of northern and central India.

Akbar's achievements were not limited to conquest. He also implemented a complex system of government that gave the Mughals smooth control of their empire. Government officials were generally paid by being given land to rule instead of a cash salary. They ruled on behalf of the emperor, raised taxes for themselves as well as for him, and raised troops for the army whenever necessary. Akbar recruited Persians and Indians into his government to balance the influence of the established Turks and Afghans, so that no one group could gain too much control.

Religious toleration

Historians have often compared Akbar with Queen Elizabeth I of England (see Unit 2, Chapter 2), who reigned in almost the same years. Both were monarchs who faced deep religious divisions in their realms but found ways to allow people of different faiths to live side by side in peace.

The Mughals were a Muslim dynasty ruling over a mostly Hindu country, and Akbar understood that this could cause conflict – especially if Hindus felt that Muslims had more power or more privileges than them. His solution was **toleration** of both religions on equal terms. Akbar abolished the **jizya** tax that non-Muslims had traditionally had to pay to their Muslim rulers, and he encouraged Hindus to continue in their religious practices without Mughal interference. He also ordered the translation of classic Hindu texts into Persian, enabling people from outside India to read the literature of Hinduism for the first time. The Muslim man who translated many of these texts, a scholar named Abd al-Qadir Badayuni, was angry at being forced to work on polytheistic religious scriptures. He responded by writing a secret, unusually critical history of Akbar's reign, published only after the emperor's death.

Akbar was a thoughtful and religious man, who took a great interest in spirituality. He was curious about all faiths, including the Catholic Christianity preached by the Portuguese who came regularly to trade in Indian ports. Eventually, Akbar tried to start his own religious order, the **Din-i Ilahi**. This was not exactly a new religion (it remained based in Islam), but it was a highly unusual religious group that presented Akbar himself as a semi-divine figure. Although it may have been designed to ensure the loyalty of India's nobles, almost nobody outside of the court converted to the Din-I Ilahi, and many were offended by it.

Akbar died in 1605. At his death he ruled over about 100 million people – more than double the entire population of Western Europe at the time.

Fact

On Akbar's coins appeared the words 'Allahu Akbar!' This is the traditional Muslim declaration 'God is great!' – but the same words could also mean 'Akbar is God!' Akbar claimed that no **blasphemy** was intended, but many suspected that he was trying to place himself at the centre of all Indian religious life.

A gold Mughal coin from the reign of Emperor Akbar (1556–1605)

Check your understanding

1. What were Akbar's main personal interests in life?
2. How did Akbar use local rulers to keep control of the territories he conquered?
3. What did Akbar do to promote peaceful co-existence between Hindus and Muslims in India?
4. What was the Din-i Ilahi?
5. What were Akbar's most important achievements as emperor of India?

Life in Mughal India

Under the Mughals, India was perhaps the richest place in the world – even though most of its people lived in poverty.

In the palaces of Mughal India, foreign visitors were dazzled by the amount of gold, silver, silk and precious jewels on display. Both the emperor and the officials around him wore dazzling costumes studded with gemstones. Palaces and massive tombs were built all over India in what became the classic Mughal architectural style – red sandstone or white marble, with remarkably intricate carvings and decorations. In the three imperial cities of Delhi, Lahore and Agra, thriving local markets sprang up in fine clothes, jewellery and expensive perfumes.

Painting of an elephant on a building in Udaipur, Rajasthan, India

It has been calculated that in the year 1700, India made up 23 per cent of the global economy, holding a massive share of the world's wealth. So where did all these riches come from?

Art in Mughal India

The wealth of the Mughal court attracted the very best artists from India, Persia and central Asia, who came hoping to find patrons for their work. Mughal painting, including the creation of illuminated manuscripts, became very famous. This tradition was Persian in origin: two major Persian painters had accompanied Humayun back to India after his time in the Safavid court, and they became the founders of Mughal painting.

Fact

The designs on Indian textiles varied according to the export destination. This is a sign that Indian clothmakers understood what would fetch a good price in different destinations around the world.

Riches through exports

Part of the reason for India's wealth was **exports**. Persian, Arab and Portuguese merchants all came to India's ports to buy Indian products, later followed by Dutch, French and British merchants. Growing commercial interest from Europeans led to an expansion of Indian industry in the 17th century. The British, who originally came to compete with the Portuguese for Indian spices, become interested in cotton **textiles**. India produced a great variety of high-quality cotton cloths, and it was soon producing even more to sell to the British. Textile and silk production in Bengal alone is estimated to have grown by a third in the hundred years before 1757 (the year when the British began conquering territory from the Mughals – see Book 3). Most of these exports were paid for in silver, so European trade was constantly injecting more silver into India.

Mughal carpet fragment from the mid-17th century

Taxation

A second source of Mughal wealth was the taxation system designed by Akbar's finance minister, Raja Todar Mal. He had commissioned surveys of India's agricultural land and calculated precisely how much of every crop should be produced in every part of the country. Todar Mal created a system that demanded maximum agricultural production.

As much as half of what a peasant produced was taken in taxes. Previously, most of this would have gone to local landowners called **zamindars**, so they too grew poorer as their incomes were redirected to the emperor. All the grain and farm products collected in taxes could then be sold, generating yet more wealth for the Mughals. The emperor and nobles used some of this money to set up schools, charitable institutions and religious houses, but they also spent much of it on their own luxurious lifestyles.

The peasants could also be called upon at any time to provide labour or military service, so they lived very insecure lives. However, Akbar had made certain reforms that did improve life, especially for women. He banned marriage for girls below the age of 14, though this was difficult to enforce. He also attempted to limit the Hindu tradition of **sati**, when a widow sacrificed herself on her husband's funeral **pyre**. Akbar also issued a decree in 1562 banning certain types of slavery, after which slavery in India became less common – though the practice did continue until the 19th century.

Caste

Since ancient times, Indian society had been divided into strict, hereditary classes called **castes**. The caste a person was born into determined what work they could do, who they could marry, and what rules they were expected to follow. It was difficult for an Indian person to live a life outside of the limits set by their caste. The four main castes, in descending order of status, were Brahmans (priests), Kshatriyas (warriors), Vaishyas (peasants) and Shudras (artisans).

A fifth main group, the Dalits ('untouchables'), were theoretically so low in status that they were not even part of the caste system. They performed work that was believed to be spiritually polluting because it brought them into contact with waste matter or dead bodies – jobs such as butchery, laundry, cleaning drains or making leather from the hides of cattle.

Check your understanding

1. Why did the production of textiles in India expand during the 17th and 18th centuries?
2. What were the main features of the taxation system devised by Raja Todar Mal?
3. How did Akbar's social reforms improve life for ordinary people in India?
4. How did the caste system divide Indian society?
5. Why was there such great inequality of wealth in Mughal India?

Jahangir and Shah Jahan

Cracks appeared in the Mughal system under the two emperors who followed Akbar, though they still extended the empire to its greatest-ever extent.

Akbar's son Prince Salim rebelled against him in 1600 and set up a rival court at Allahabad. When Akbar sent his official biographer Abu al-Fazl to negotiate with him, Salim had him murdered. The two were reconciled shortly before Akbar's death, but Salim had demonstrated his hunger for power. When he became emperor in 1605, he took the name Jahangir, which means 'World-Seizer'.

Jahangir, the fourth Mughal emperor

Jahangir was an alcoholic, and his addiction may have made it difficult for him to take an active part in ruling. For much of his reign, power was held by his wife, Nur Jahan ('Light of the World'). She issued royal decrees in her name and commanded armies in battle, riding atop a war elephant – on one occasion, she rescued Jahangir after he was captured by rebels. She even issued coins bearing her name, a practice usually reserved for emperors.

During Jahangir's reign, his son Khurram began a great campaign to conquer the **Deccan Plateau**, a vast highland plain in southern India that remained outside of Mughal control. The Deccan was fragmented among several local rulers, but it was a hard land to conquer, partly because of the rocky and mountainous terrain. Khurram also found himself facing a particularly powerful and skilful enemy.

Malik Ambar was an African man who had been sold into slavery in Baghdad and brought to the Deccan. He soon proved himself a great military commander, earned his freedom, and rose to become ruler of the Ahmadnagar sultanate – one of the largest states in the Deccan. Malik Ambar copied many of Raja Todar Mal's tax reforms, hoping to draw as much money from his lands as the Mughals did from theirs. Under Malik Ambar, elite cavalry units were formed from the local Hindu aristocracy, who would become a devastating foe to Mughal armies. These mounted warriors were called the **Marathas**.

In 1625, Khurram asked Malik Ambar to join him in an alliance against Jahangir, so that Khurram could seize the Mughal throne. Malik Ambar agreed, and the two of them won several victories against Mughal forces loyal to Jahangir, before Malik Ambar died in 1626. A year later, Jahangir also died, and Khurram was well prepared to take power. He won a brief war against his brothers, became emperor in 1628, and took the name Shah Jahan – 'King of the World'.

Nur Jahan holding a portrait of Emperor Jahangir

Shah Jahan

As emperor, Shah Jahan was determined to expand the Mughal empire even further. He fought a series of unsuccessful wars against the Safavid Persian empire to the west, spending vast sums of money to capture territory that he lost after only a few years. He had more success in the Deccan as he continued the Mughal takeover of the plateau. By 1636 he had conquered Malik Ambar's old sultanate, Ahmadnagar, but huge areas of the Deccan remained outside of Mughal rule.

Shah Jahan also had a passion for architecture, and many of the greatest buildings of Mughal India were built in his reign. He built a vast palace in Delhi called the Red Fort, and a similar one in Agra. Most famously, Shah Jahan built the **Taj Mahal**, which stands in Agra and is often said to be the most beautiful building in the world. It was built as a tomb for his beloved wife, Mumtaz Mahal, who was one of his closest and most trusted advisors. She died in 1631 while giving birth to their 14th child.

The Taj Mahal in Agra, Uttar Pradesh. The ivory-white marble mausoleum was built between 1632 and 1648

Sikhism

A Sikh man

During the Mughal period, a new religion called **Sikhism** slowly gathered followers in India. Sikhism originated in India's northern Punjab region during the late 15th century, drawing inspiration from both Islam and Hinduism. Its founder, **Guru** Nanak, taught a doctrine based on the unity of the divine and the equality of all believers regardless of caste. He argued that both Hindu and Muslim elites and priesthoods were working to divide humanity by making people believe that the one God is not for everyone. Guru Nanak was the first in a sequence of ten gurus who guided the early Sikhs. The tenth died in 1708 after naming the Sikh scripture, rather than another person, as his successor.

After Akbar's time, Sikhs often came into conflict with the Mughal authorities. Jahangir executed Guru Arjan, the fifth guru of Sikhism, because he was thought to have supported a rebellion by Jahangir's son Khusrau. In 1675, Shah Jahan's successor Aurangzeb executed Guru Tegh Bahadur, the ninth guru, after hearing reports of Muslims converting to Sikhism. The guru's three closest followers were killed along with him: one sawn in half, one burned alive, and one plunged into boiling water. The tenth guru, Guru Gobind Singh, re-organised the Sikh community to create a highly disciplined fighting force, so that they could resist Mughal power. Sikh rebellion in the Punjab became a recurring problem for the later Mughal emperors.

Check your understanding

1. What was Nur Jahan's role in the Mughal government?
2. What made Malik Ambar such a formidable opponent for Khurram?
3. What were Shah Jahan's achievements as emperor?
4. Why did the Sikh community in India eventually turn against their Mughal rulers?
5. Why did attempts to conquer the Deccan prove so difficult for the Mughal emperors?

Unit 9: Mughal India
Decline of the Mughals

During the late 17th century, the Mughal empire grew weaker under the rule of the emperor Aurangzeb. By the early 18th century, the empire was well past the height of its power.

Shah Jahan had four sons. By Mughal tradition, all four had an equal right to rule the kingdom, so conflict between them was almost inevitable. Shah Jahan's eldest and favourite son, Dara Shikoh, was a brilliant scholar who personally translated many Hindu religious texts into Persian. He also wanted to continue Akbar's project of working for understanding between Hindus and Muslims. Shah Jahan wanted Dara Shikoh to inherit the empire, but this offended his third son, the ambitious Aurangzeb, who was Shah Jahan's governor of the Deccan Plateau (see Chapter 4, this unit). When Shah Jahan fell ill in 1657, war broke out between his sons.

Aurangzeb allied with his youngest brother, Murad, to defeat the other two brothers. Yet, after winning a decisive victory at the Battle of Samugarh, Aurangzeb betrayed Murad and had him executed. He then imprisoned his sick father in Agra while the two defeated brothers, Shuja and Dara Shikoh, fled separately into exile. Shuja disappeared in the kingdom of Arakan, in what is now Myanmar, and was never seen again. Meanwhile, Dara Shikoh was given refuge by an Afghan chieftan, who then betrayed him and sent him back to Delhi in chains. Aurangzeb had Dara Shikoh publicly executed and sent his severed head to his imprisoned father Shah Jahan.

Shah Jahan lived as a prisoner in Agra until his death in 1666. Aurangzeb, meanwhile, became the sixth Mughal emperor of India.

Aurangzeb, Mughal emperor from 1658 to 1707. He was considered an accomplished but controversial ruler

The reign of Aurangzeb

Under Aurangzeb, Mughal power came under serious strain. Part of the reason was a long-term rise in peasant rebellion and rural banditry, as the empire's severe tax regime caused many ordinary people to abandon their land and turn to violence in order to survive. Furthermore, Aurangzeb made things worse through his religious policy and his unsuccessful wars.

Aurangzeb was a deeply pious Muslim, and some of his policies caused anger among Hindus. He restored the jizya tax on non-Muslims, doubled the taxes on Hindu merchants while abolishing them for Muslim merchants, and attempted to ban the consumption of alcohol. However, Aurangzeb mostly continued the established policy of religious toleration and did not attempt to suppress or persecute Hindus; indeed, the proportion of Hindus in government jobs rose during his reign.

A more serious problem for the empire was Aurangzeb's long series of military failures. Throughout his reign, Aurangzeb was obsessively focused on completing the conquest of the Deccan Plateau. His main enemies were the Marathas, who by 1674 formed an independent kingdom of their own. They were brought together by a warrior king named Shivaji, who is remembered to this day as a hero by some Hindus. Shivaji led a life of daring adventure and was renowned as a brilliant general. He prided himself on protecting Hinduism, but he also practised religious toleration, allowing Muslims to live in peace in the Maratha kingdom.

Shivaji died in 1680, but his son Sambhaji continued the struggle against Aurangzeb. In 1682 Aurangzeb personally moved south to take up command of the Deccan war himself, but he made very little progress. The mountainous, rocky region known as the Western Ghats, where the Marathas had their strongholds, was full of ravines and forests – unsuited to the large Mughal armies. Aurangzeb's failed campaigns were vastly expensive and left the empire weak and short of manpower elsewhere.

Statue of King Shivaji at Raigad Fort, Maharashtra, India

Europeans in India

During the reign of Aurangzeb, the European trading stations on the Indian coast began to get drawn into local conflicts. Sambhaji attacked the Portuguese base at Goa in 1683 because Aurangzeb was using it to supply his armies. Increasingly, it seemed that these bases would need armed protection. One English merchant wrote to his employers in London that "the times now require you to manage your general commerce with your sword in your hands".

Aurangzeb fought the Marathas right up until his death in 1707 – aged 88, which was unusually old. When he died, his sons immediately began to fight over the throne. Rebellions broke out in multiple parts of the Mughal Empire, including the old Rajput states and the Sikh region of the Punjab. These rebellions were suppressed, but it was clear that Mughal power was a shadow of what it had once been.

The Mughal empire would in theory last for another 150 years, but it never recovered the stability it had experienced under Akbar, Jahangir and Shah Jahan. Instead, local princes became all but independent in practice, while the emperors in Delhi exercised less and less real control. As the 18th century went on, the weakness of the Mughal empire made it increasingly easy for Europeans – above all the British – to claim power in India.

Check your understanding

1. How did Aurangzeb overpower his father and brothers to become emperor of India?

2. Why was peasant rebellion and banditry on the rise in India?

3. What were Aurangzeb's religious policies?

4. Why did Aurangzeb fail to complete the conquest of the Deccan?

5. Why was the Mughal empire in serious decline by the end of Aurangzeb's reign?

Unit 9: Mughal India
Knowledge organiser

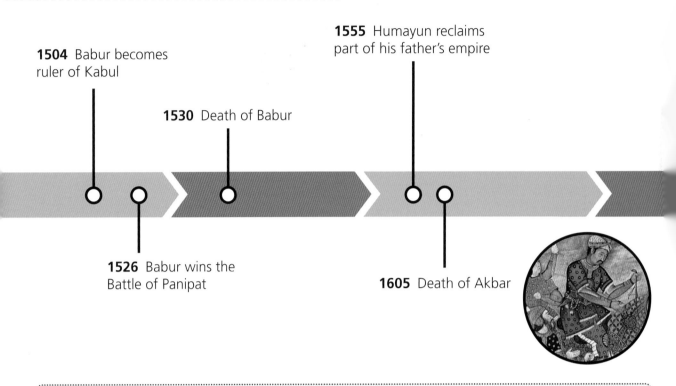

1504 Babur becomes ruler of Kabul

1530 Death of Babur

1555 Humayun reclaims part of his father's empire

1526 Babur wins the Battle of Panipat

1605 Death of Akbar

Key vocabulary

Caste A hereditary class that determines a person's status and options in life

Blasphemy Speech that causes religious offence

Deccan Plateau A very large highland region that covers much of southern India

Delhi Major city in northern India that was the Mughal capital

Din-i Ilahi Religious order founded by Akbar, based in Islam but promoting Akbar himself as a semi-divine figure

Exports Goods or services sold to other countries

Ferghana Valley Region in present-day Uzbekistan, in central Asia, that was Babur's home kingdom

Guru A highly respected and influential teacher, usually on religious or spiritual matters

Jizya Tax on non-Muslims living in Muslim lands

Kabul City in Afghanistan that became Babur's capital

Marathas People native to the Deccan who formed an independent kingdom in the 17th century and fought the Mughals

Mughals Dynasty originally from central Asia that ruled much of India from the 16th to 19th centuries

Punjab The north-western region of India

Pyre Fire on which a body is burned at a funeral

Raja Indian word for king

Rajput states Small kingdoms in northern India before the Mughal conquest, ruled by Hindu princes

Regent Someone who is appointed to rule on behalf of a monarch, when the monarch is too young, infirm or absent to rule

Safavid empire Persian empire that was Mughal India's most powerful neighbour

Sati The Hindu custom of widows sacrificing themselves on their husband's funeral pyre

Sikhism Religion that arose in India in the 15th century and became a major force in the Mughal period

Sultanate An Islamic kingdom ruled by a sultan

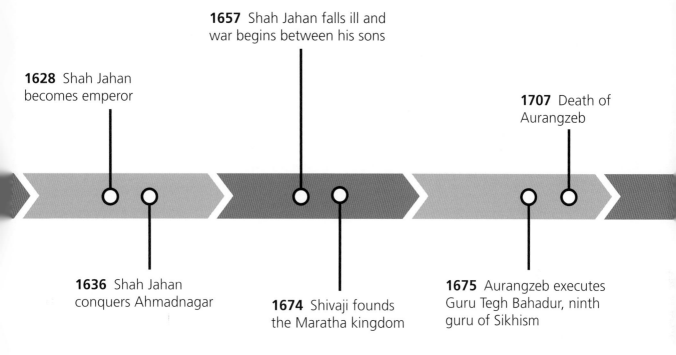

1657 Shah Jahan falls ill and war begins between his sons

1628 Shah Jahan becomes emperor

1707 Death of Aurangzeb

1636 Shah Jahan conquers Ahmadnagar

1674 Shivaji founds the Maratha kingdom

1675 Aurangzeb executes Guru Tegh Bahadur, ninth guru of Sikhism

Key people

Akbar Third Mughal emperor of India, often considered the country's greatest ruler

Aurangzeb Sixth Mughal emperor of India, who weakened the empire by his long campaigns in the Deccan Plateau

Babur First Mughal emperor of India, who was driven out of central Asia before conquering much of northern India

Humayun Second Mughal emperor of India, who lost his empire and fled to Safavid Persia

Jahangir Fourth Mughal emperor of India (formerly Prince Salim)

Nur Jahan Ruler of India in practice for much of the reign of Jahangir, her husband

Shah Jahan Fifth Mughal emperor of India (formerly Prince Khurram), who built the Taj Mahal

Shivaji Warrior king of the Marathas, who fought Aurangzeb and is still remembered as a hero by many Hindus

Key vocabulary

Taj Mahal Tomb of Shah Jahan's wife Mumtaz Mahal, often said to be the most beautiful building in the world

Textiles Cloth and woven fabrics

Toleration The policy, or practice, of allowing diverse beliefs and opinions without enforcing any one ideology

Zamindars Local landowners in India, richer than peasants but without the status or privileges of nobles

The Tokugawa shogunate

During the 16th century, Japan was divided between many different clans. Then a series of powerful warlords united the country under their rule.

There was an emperor in Kyoto, in central Japan, who in theory ruled all of Japan, but in practice his role had become symbolic. He no longer held much actual power over the many regional Japanese lords, known as **daimyo**. These lords fought each other constantly, and ordinary Japanese people were forced to live with prolonged civil war.

The unification of Japan

In 1583, a powerful daimyo named Toyotomi Hideyoshi began a campaign of unification. Hideyoshi had a major advantage: his armies used firearms. Guns had recently been brought to Japan by Portuguese traders, though the Japanese quickly learned how to manufacture guns themselves.

Hideyoshi successfully brought most of Japan under his control. He wanted to regulate Japanese society to avoid disruption and ensure lasting peace. In 1588, he supervised a great 'sword hunt' to take weapons away from all those who were not **samurai** warriors (see box). He also created a strict division of Japanese society into four classes: the samurai at the top, then the peasant farmers, then artisans, then merchants. Peasants, who made up about 80 per cent of the population, were ranked second because of the importance of rice-growing, while merchants were at the bottom because commerce and trade were seen as dishonourable work.

In 1592, Hideyoshi decided he wished to become emperor of China. To get there, he launched an invasion of Korea, beginning a disastrous series of campaigns that ended with his death in 1598. Hideyoshi left a five-year-old son as his heir, but somebody else was waiting to seize control.

Tokugawa Ieyasu was a mighty daimyo who had pledged his loyalty to Hideyoshi in 1585. He was a patient man who worked steadily to build up his own power while serving his lord. By the time of Hideyoshi's death, Ieyasu had the largest army and the most productive lands in Japan, making him ideally placed to take over the system that Hideyoshi had built.

On 21 October 1600, Ieyasu's army fought the remaining followers of Hideyoshi, now led by a daimyo named Ishida Mitsunari. The **Battle of Sekigahara** decided the political

Tokugawa Ieyasu (1543–1616), founder and first shogun of the Tokugawa shogunate of Japan

future of Japan, because Ieyasu's victory gave him near-total control of the country. In 1603, the emperor officially recognised Ieyasu as **shogun** – a military overlord with the right to govern Japan on the emperor's behalf. This was the beginning of the Tokugawa **shogunate**, the regime that would rule Japan for the next 250 years.

This era of Japanese history is sometimes called the Tokugawa period, after its rulers. More commonly, it is known as the **Edo** period – named after Tokugawa Ieyasu's base at the city of Edo. The Tokugawa clan was the biggest landowner and richest family, controlling the main cities and much of Japan's rice-growing land. The several hundred lesser daimyo owed loyalty to the shogun in exchange for order and protection – a system similar to that in feudal medieval Europe. To ensure their loyalty, all daimyo were required to spend alternate years living in Edo and in their own **domains**, while their wives and children lived permanently in Edo. This meant their families were effectively kept as hostages. Even so, not all daimyo could be trusted, and the shoguns had to be constantly alert to the threat of rebellion.

Samurai

Japan's hereditary class of warriors were called the samurai. They were highly skilled swordsmen who lived by a strict moral code called **bushido**, 'the way of the warrior'. A samurai carried two swords, symbols of his authority, which he was permitted to use on commoners who did not show him respect. The samurai sword, called a **katana**, was a beautifully crafted object regarded not only as a weapon but as a work of art.

A samurai was sworn to serve his lord with the utmost loyalty, including by sacrificing his own life if necessary. If a samurai had been disgraced, or if he wished to avoid dishonour following defeat in battle, he might commit **seppuku** – ritual suicide by slicing open his own stomach with a katana. If a samurai was masterless (usually because his lord had died without an heir), he became a **ronin**: a wandering warrior, who might look for a new master or, sometimes, work as a **mercenary**.

Before the Tokugawa period, non-samurai could sometimes rise to become samurai themselves. There was even a Black African man, named Yasuke, who became a samurai after coming to Japan with an Italian mission in 1579.

Samurai armour and katana on display in the British Museum, London

Fact

Female warriors named *onna-musha* also fought alongside samurai men. They used a weapon called the *naginata*, a long pole with a curved blade.

Check your understanding

1. Who held power in Japan before the rise of Toyotomi Hideyoshi?

2. How did Hideyoshi attempt to regulate Japanese society?

3. Why was Tokugawa Ieyasu in a good position to take power when Hideyoshi died?

4. What values were important to samurai warriors?

5. How did Tokugawa Ieyasu take and keep control of Japan?

Unit 10: Edo Japan
A closed country

The Tokugawa shogunate enforced a remarkable policy that meant that Japan was almost totally sealed off from the rest of the world.

The Portuguese were the first European visitors to Japan, around 1543. They originally came seeking to buy silver, which was abundant in Japan, for which they traded firearms, textiles and new crops from the Americas such as sugar. However, soon afterwards Catholic **missionaries** from the **Jesuit** order arrived, hoping to convert the Japanese to Christianity. The first Jesuit mission to Japan arrived in 1549 and was headed by Francis Xavier, who was one of the seven original members of the order and had also worked to spread Christianity in India.

Japanese painting of a visiting European ship by Kanō Naizen, c.1600

According to Jesuit sources, Christianity spread rapidly in Japan, such that by 1600 there may have been around half a million Japanese Christians in a country of 18 million people. To Japan's new rulers, this foreign ideology seemed disruptive and threatening. Toyotomi Hideyoshi had 26 Christians crucified in 1597 after they claimed the King of Spain was planning to invade Japan. They immediately became famous Catholic martyrs. This marked the beginning of the persecution of Japanese Christians.

Tokugawa Ieyasu originally wished to preserve and even expand foreign trade, which he saw as a source of valuable goods and information about the world. However, he soon realised that trade and Christianity could not be separated. Ieyasu also feared that open trade in firearms could empower his enemies, and that Christians would ally with rebel daimyo against him. Most foreign trade came through Japan's south-western ports, which also happened to be in the domains ruled by the most hostile daimyo, who were most likely to rise in rebellion. In 1613, Ieyasu issued a decree banning Christianity, and began his attempt to close Japan to foreign contact.

Fushimi Inari Shrine, an important Shinto shrine in southern Kyoto

Japanese religions

The traditional Japanese religion is called **Shinto**, but it was not treated as a unified religion until the 19th century. Before then, Shinto was more like a collection of local cults sharing some common characteristics, mostly centred on shrines and involving relations with spirits called kami. These cults co-existed with organised Buddhism, which had much more formal institutions and teachings.

Closing Japan

Between 1633 and 1639, Tokugawa Iemitsu, who was Ieyasu's grandson and the third Tokugawa shogun, issued a series of decrees that created a system restricting foreigners from coming to Japan. Under this policy, Japanese people were forbidden from leaving Japan, and those already overseas were forbidden to return. The building of ocean-going ships was banned, and all Japanese people were required to register at a Buddhist temple.

Most importantly, almost all foreigners were banned from freely entering Japan – only the Dutch and the Chinese were allowed to enter. The Dutch were restricted to a tiny artificial island in **Nagasaki** harbour known as **Dejima**. Two Dutch ships per year were allowed to visit this trading post, and no more. The shogunate made an exception for the Dutch because they swore not to preach Christianity, and because their agents were willing to trample on the cross as a symbolic act. (It helped that the Dutch were Protestants, so were not associated with Jesuit missionary work.) Chinese merchants, who were seen as less dangerous because Chinese culture was more familiar to the Japanese, were also restricted to Nagasaki. Other than the strictly controlled trade through this one port, almost all foreign contact with Japan was now at an end.

The Shimabara Rebellion

In 1637, on Kyushu (the southernmost of Japan's four large islands), there was a rebellion against poverty and social oppression, led by a Christian rebel named Amakusa Shiro. The **Shimabara Rebellion** frightened the shogunate and made Iemitsu determined to crack down even harder on Christianity. Thousands were forced to renounce Christianity or be martyred (killed for their religious beliefs).

Fact

When a Portuguese embassy arrived in 1640 to formally request permission to re-enter Japan, most of its members were killed for their Catholic faith.

The impact of restrictions

Japan was a self-sufficient country that produced most of what it needed, so it did not need to trade extensively to survive. The shogunate also learned about what was happening in the wider world through regular reports compiled by the Dutch, an important condition of their trade. However, shutting off most connections to the outside world had profound effects on Japanese society – it meant that new ideas, belief systems, technologies and fashions could rarely enter.

The policy of closing Japan to foreign influence also meant that the shogunate could control the country more closely and suppress rebellion, while continuing to make money through controlled overseas trade. The Tokugawa clan presided over a remarkably long period of stability that lasted for over two centuries – the '**Great Peace**'. On the other hand, some historians argue that the limitation of outside contact discouraged change and allowed a socially rigid class system to survive in Japan for much longer than similar social systems in Europe. Finally, it meant that when foreigners did at last return to Japan in the 19th century, the country was poorly prepared to respond to their challenge.

Check your understanding:

1. Why did Europeans come to Japan in the 16th century?
2. What were the effects of the decrees passed by Tokugawa Iemitsu between 1633 and 1639?
3. What conditions were set on Dutch trade in Japan after the 1630s?
4. Why do historians disagree about the impacts of the policy of restricting foreign access?
5. Why did the Tokugawa shoguns impose the policy of restricting foreign access?

Unit 10: Edo Japan
The Great Peace

Compared with most of the world in the 17th and 18th centuries, living standards in Edo Japan were remarkably high. Income and life expectancy for the average person were comparable with those in Britain.

Tokugawa rule put an end to the warfare that had troubled Japan for centuries, and it allowed ordinary people to live in peace (despite occasional peasant uprisings). One immediate consequence was rising food production, which in turn led to a growing population and new wealth. The Tokugawa policy of gathering daimyo and samurai in the major cities, rather than letting them live on rural estates as was traditional, encouraged merchants to move to these cities to provide for them. With all the richest people concentrated in a few places, business boomed and these cities swelled. By 1750, Osaka and Kyoto had around 300 000 people each, while the capital, Edo, had over a million.

Osaka Castle in Osaka. Construction of the castle was completed in 1597

Basic education became common. By the 19th century, most Japanese people were at least partially literate, and there was a big market for printed books. As commercial activity spread even to the smallest villages, close transport and communication links developed between all areas of the country.

Despite these transformations, the basic values in Japanese society remained unchanged. Japanese morality was taught in Buddhist temples, and was based on duty, honour and respect for social superiors. Within a family, everyone was expected to show absolute obedience to the head of the household. Men were expected to hold authority and women were expected to submit to it. Nevertheless, women could sometimes control their own possessions, and initiate divorce.

Culture and the arts

The Edo period is usually remembered as a time of great achievements in Japanese culture. The traditional Japanese arts, such as flower arranging, the tea ceremony and *noh* theatre, all continued to flourish. There were also many new innovations. In the late 17th century, **haiku** poetry appeared in Japan, pioneered by the poet Matsuo Basho; it remains a popular form of poetry to this day. The traditional technique of woodblock printing was refined until it could produce beautiful and striking images, many of which later became famous around the world – such as those by the early 19th-century printmaker Hokusai Katsushika.

In the very early 1600s, a woman named Okuni gathered an all-female troupe of actors, dancers and singers, and began staging extravagant performances involving music, dance and storytelling. This was the origin of **kabuki** theatre, which differed from the traditional noh theatre in being aimed at the common people rather than the elite. Okuni's shows were funny, raunchy and designed as popular entertainment. Conservative Japanese found them scandalous, particularly as many of the performers were often also sex workers. In 1629, Tokugawa Iemitsu banned women from the stage, meaning that only men could perform in *kabuki*.

Class and status

The four-tier class system created by Toyotomi Hideyoshi lasted throughout the Tokugawa period. Detailed **sumptuary laws** defined what each of the four classes could wear and how they could be seen in public, keeping them strictly and visibly separated. However, the shogunate tolerated the opening of 'floating worlds': districts where class rules were suspended and people were mostly free to behave as they pleased. As time went on the class system also bore less and less relation to real divisions in wealth. Merchants, theoretically the lowest of the four classes, could now become richer than many samurai. Some peasants even became rich landowners. To the samurai, this seemed deeply troubling, as their elite social position was threatened.

A kabuki theatre performance. To this day, only men are allowed to be kabuki performers

The samurai relied on the rice tax for their income. Most taxes in Edo Japan were collected not in money but in *koku* of rice (one *koku* was the amount of rice that a single person consumed in a year). However, the assessments of how much rice should come from each area of land had been set by Toyotomi Hideyoshi and were almost never updated, even when farmers opened new 'secret fields'. This meant that even as Japan grew more prosperous, the rice tax did not rise. Merchants' incomes, based on thriving commerce, far outstripped the incomes of many samurai.

The samurai were also left without their traditional social role to fill. Their skills as warriors were no longer needed in the Great Peace, and they were sometimes poorer than lower-status people. They still studied the sword, but most never fought except to train. Some took an interest in philosophy, science and literature. Others took jobs in the government and became administrators, but there were so many samurai (the class formed about 6 per cent of the population) that the shogunate could only provide jobs for around a quarter of them. Some samurai even began working as merchants, abandoning the traditional values of their class.

Fact

In 1681, the shogun Tokugawa Tsunayoshi observed a magnificently dressed woman and enquired after her, assuming that she was the wife of a daimyo. It turned out that she was the wife of a merchant named Ishikawa Rokubee. The shogun was furious that Rokubee's family were breaking the sumptuary laws. He confiscated all Rokubee's property and banished his family from Edo.

Check your understanding:

1. Why did Tokugawa rule lead to the expansion of Japan's cities?
2. What were the traditional values in a Japanese family?
3. Why were women banned from the stage in the 17th century?
4. Why did many samurai in the Edo period become poorer than those of lower social status?
5. How did the Great Peace create changes that disrupted traditional Japanese society?

Western encounters

In the 19th century, powers such as France, Russia and the USA all began to take a closer interest in Japan. They suspected that trading there would be very profitable, and they wanted the country opened.

During the Great Peace, which lasted for most of the Tokugawa era, some Japanese people continued to take an interest in the outside world, especially China and the West. Yet, learning about the world beyond Japan remained difficult. Chinese books could be imported, but the ban on Christianity meant that people were wary of obtaining European books, which were expensive anyway because so few of them could be bought from the Dutch in their twice-yearly visits to Nagasaki.

All the same, enough European books got into Japan for a few daimyo to establish centres of 'Dutch Studies' – schools for learning about the West. Japanese craftsmen also studied and learned the secrets of whatever inventions did arrive from Europe, and they were soon able to manufacture clocks or scientific instruments with just as much precision as anyone outside Japan. Curiosity about the world beyond Japan was intensifying.

> **Fact**
>
> In 1774 a translation of a Dutch anatomy textbook was published in Japan. It sparked a surge in medical research.

European curiosity about life within Japan was also growing, and outside attempts to contact people in Japan grew bolder. In the early 19th century, there were Russian landings on Sakhalin and the Kuril Islands, which lie to the north of Japan. British ships also began sailing through Japanese waters. In response, in 1825 the shogunate renewed a decree known as the 'no second thought' law, whereby any foreigner who came ashore must be immediately arrested or killed.

In 1842, the British inflicted a humiliating defeat on China during the First Opium War, forcing China to let them trade in many Chinese ports that had previously been closed. The Tokugawa government observed these events with serious concern. Clearly, the Western powers now had enough military strength to force an Asian country to accept them as trading partners. What was to stop them doing the same to Japan?

Commodore Perry's mission

Very soon afterwards, the United States sent a mission to pressure Japan into opening its ports. Commodore Matthew Perry was sent to Japan by the US government to force the country to accept American trade. On 8 July 1853 he sailed into Edo Bay with a squadron of four warships, unannounced and uninvited. When the shogunate refused to answer his demands, he agreed to wait – but said he would return the following spring to demand a response.

Engraving of Commodore Perry of the Japan Expedition, dated 1854

Unsure what to do, the shogun's government took the unprecedented step of asking for advice from all of the daimyo. The shogun at the time, Tokugawa Iesada, was sickly and uninterested in ruling. Many of the lords took the request for advice as a signal that the Tokugawa family no longer held real authority, as they seemed unable to come up with a response to the American threat. The more rebellious daimyo began actively preparing to push for independence from the shogun.

When Perry returned in 1854 with a fleet of nine warships, the shogunate reluctantly signed a treaty allowing American ships to dock in Japanese ports. A US ambassador, Townsend Harris, was admitted to the country, and he began pressuring the shogunate to accept American trade. The Tokugawa politicians, led by an official named Ii Naosuke, feared the consequences of defying American power. In 1858 they agreed to accept US trade. Immediately, the other Western powers that were active in East Asia – Britain, Russia, the Netherlands and France – also demanded trading rights. Japan ended up signing treaties with all five nations, a series of agreements known as the Ansei Treaties.

Portrait of Ii Naosuke, painted by his son

These treaties were designed to give the foreigners the advantage in all future trade. Western merchants and visitors who committed crimes in Japan would be outside of Japanese law and could not be tried in Japanese courts. Japan was also forced to accept low import and export duties, some as low as 5 per cent, meaning that the trade would be profitable to the foreigners but not to the Japanese government. For these reasons, the Ansei Treaties were also known as the 'unequal treaties'. Most restrictions on contact with foreigners were abolished, and it seemed that Japan was indeed suffering the same fate as China.

A debate began in the court of the shogun: should Japan accept the end of its isolation and try to make the most of it? Or should it begin developing its military power until it could defend itself against the West? There was no agreement, but in the end it did not matter what the politicians decided: the surrender of trading rights to the foreigners caused great anger in Japan. Rebel daimyo felt that the Tokugawa shogunate no longer deserved their loyalty, and many samurai began pressing their lords to overthrow the regime.

Check your understanding

1. How did some knowledge from the outside world spread in Japan even during the Sakoku period?
2. Why did the events of the First Opium War cause anxiety in Japan?
3. Why did Commodore Matthew Perry come to Japan?
4. What were the conditions of the Ansei Treaties?
5. Why did the Tokugawa shogunate accept trade with Western nations in the late 1850s?

The Meiji Restoration

The Edo period came to an end with a profound transformation. It was called the Meiji Restoration, and it completely reshaped Japanese society, giving birth to a mighty modern nation.

To gather support from the common people, some of the rebel daimyo realised that they could appeal to the symbolic power of the emperor. Because the shoguns theoretically ruled on the emperor's behalf, the rebels could claim that by giving in to the foreigners, the Tokugawa government had given away the emperor's power. This was a powerful claim in a country where many people felt deep respect for the emperors. 'Revere the emperor and expel the barbarians!' became a common anti-Tokugawa slogan.

In 1860, Ii Naosuke was assassinated by men from the rebel domains of Mito and Satsuma. This was revenge for his role in the signing of the Ansei Treaties. From this point on, the rebel daimyo openly defied Tokugawa authority. There was some rivalry among the rebels, but in 1866 the two leading rebel domains, Satsuma and Choshu, formed an alliance. There was now little hope for the shogunate.

In the same year, Tokugawa Yoshinobu became shogun – a man of much greater intelligence and energy than his recent predecessors. He was determined to keep his family in power, but his options were very limited. In 1867, Yoshinobu formally handed power back to the emperor, giving up the Tokugawa family's position as shoguns. He knew that the rebels would not accept Tokugawa rule any longer, and he hoped that this move would at least allow his clan to retain some dominance. However, the rebels argued that so long as the Tokugawa family controlled over a quarter of Japanese land, they would still hold too much power.

In January 1868, a samurai named Saigo Takamori, who was one of the rebel leaders, seized the emperor's palace in Kyoto with a handful of troops. The rebels now declared a full 'restoration' of imperial power (the term is not strictly accurate, as the emperors had not held real power even before the Tokugawa period). The Tokugawa, they said, would be completely excluded from their new government. Although Yoshinobu accepted the outcome, some of his Tokugawa followers insisted on fighting. The rebel forces – now calling themselves 'imperial' forces – beat the Tokugawa army at the Battle of Toba-Fushimi, and then captured Edo itself. The shogunate was no more.

National transformation

The emperor in 1868 was a 15-year-old boy who took the **regnal name** Meiji. For the first time in centuries, he was now given a real political role. The four greatest clans – Satsuma, Choshu, Tosa and Hizen – all

Emperor Meiji of Japan

surrendered their lands to the emperor. They did this, they declared, so that Japan would be united and strong, not weakened by conflicts between regional lords. All other daimyo followed suit, and Japan was formally united as a single legal domain for the first time. Japan became an **oligarchy** ruled by a small group of powerful politicians in close alliance with the emperor. The imperial court was moved from Kyoto to Edo, and Edo was renamed Tokyo.

The new regime wanted to transform Japan into a modern, industrial power that could deal on equal terms with the nations of the West. They immediately began establishing modern institutions and practices copied from the Europeans and Americans. In the first five years alone, they set up a modern **civil service**, a postal service, military conscription and railways. The four-class social system was abolished, religious toleration was introduced, and factories were built all over the country.

Japan was on the 'fast track' to modernisation. This was a revolution by the elite, but most Japanese people accepted and supported it. They had observed the ongoing exploitation of China by the Western powers, which had only grown worse since the First Opium War. The Japanese people wanted their country to be a great power in the world – a nation strong enough that it could, if necessary, stand up to Western empires in war.

The Satsuma Rebellion

When the samurai lost their privileges as a class, many of those who had taken part in the Meiji Restoration were angry. This was not the future they had wanted. One of these former samurai was Saigo Takamori. He had been one of the leaders of the revolution and was seen as a founder of the new Japan, but he had wanted a return to traditional Japanese life, not a transformation into something new and modern.

> **Fact**
>
> The satsuma fruit is named after the province of Japan that also gives its name to the rebellion.

In 1877, Saigo led a rebellion against the new regime, with thousands of former samurai flocking to his cause. However, these traditional warriors, armed with swords and rifles, could not stand up to the technologically advanced Japanese army. The **Satsuma Rebellion** (named after the region of Japan where it took place) was crushed. This is often seen as the last stand of the old Japan. It proved that there would be no going back to the days of the Tokugawa, or anything before them.

Saigo Takamori committing seppuku (ritual suicide by disembowelment) during the Satsuma Rebellion (the actual circumstances of his death are unknown)

Check your understanding

1. Why did rebel daimyo begin appealing to the emperor to oppose the Tokugawa shogunate?
2. How did Tokugawa Yoshinobu attempt to keep his family in power?
3. Who made up the new government that took power in Japan in 1868?
4. Why did Saigo Takamori lead a rebellion against the new regime in 1877?
5. What were key objectives of Japan's government following the Meiji Restoration?

Unit 10: Edo Japan
Knowledge organiser

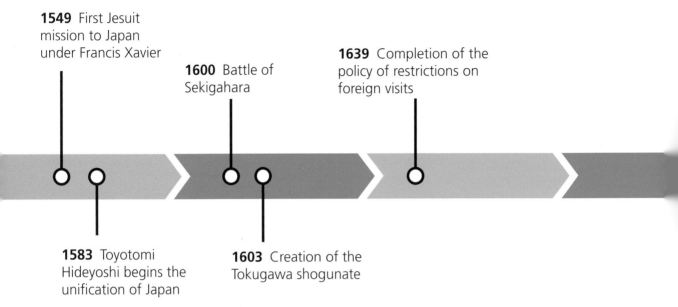

1549 First Jesuit mission to Japan under Francis Xavier

1600 Battle of Sekigahara

1639 Completion of the policy of restrictions on foreign visits

1583 Toyotomi Hideyoshi begins the unification of Japan

1603 Creation of the Tokugawa shogunate

Key vocabulary

Battle of Sekigahara Decisive victory for Tokugawa Ieyasu against followers of the Toyotomi

Bushido The moral code followed by samurai, meaning 'the way of the warrior'

Civil service The permanent staff of a government, responsible for overseeing the business of the country

Daimyo Regional lords in medieval and Edo Japan

Dejima Artificial island in Nagasaki harbour, used by the Dutch as the only legal trading post for Europeans in Edo Japan

Domain The estate of a daimyo and the main administrative division in Edo Japan

Edo City (now named Tokyo) that was the unofficial capital of the Tokugawa shogunate, giving its name to the period

Great Peace Name commonly given to the two-century period of stability and peace in Japan under the Tokugawa shogunate

Haiku Short form of poetry consisting of a five-syllable line, a seven-syllable line, and then another five-syllable line

Jesuits Elite Catholic order that carried out missionary work all over the world during the

Early Modern period. Their religious fanaticism sometimes resulted in violence against non-Catholics

Kabuki Form of Japanese theatre developed in early Edo times and aimed at a popular audience

Katana Sword used by samurai

Meiji Restoration Political and social transformation in which the Tokugawa shogunate was overthrown and a government by the emperor and leading noble families was established

Mercenary Professional soldier who fights for anyone who pays them

Missionaries People who go out to spread their religion to others, particularly in a foreign country

Nagasaki Major port city in south-west Japan, where Dutch and Chinese trade was permitted during the period of international restrictions

Oligarchy Government by a small group of people, often members of a rich elite

Regnal name Name taken by a king or emperor while on the throne, which is different from their personal name

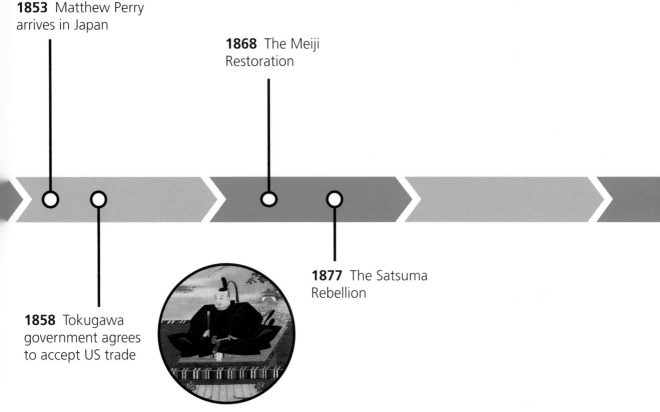

1853 Matthew Perry arrives in Japan

1868 The Meiji Restoration

1858 Tokugawa government agrees to accept US trade

1877 The Satsuma Rebellion

Key vocabulary

Ronin A samurai without a master, who might wander or work as a mercenary

Samurai Japan's hereditary class of warriors, who became government administrators in the Edo period

Satsuma Rebellion Uprising by discontented samurai hoping to reverse the Meiji Restoration

Seppuku Ritual suicide performed by samurai, done by slicing open the stomach with a katana

Shimabara Rebellion Rebellion involving Japanese Christians in 1637

Shinto The traditional Japanese religion, formed from a collection of local practices and beliefs

Shogun A warlord who ruled Japan on behalf of the emperor

Shogunate Military government head by a shogun

Sumptuary laws Rules explaining what clothing different ranks in society could wear

Key people

Francis Xavier Leader of the first Jesuit missionary to Japan

Matthew Perry US naval officer who attempted to force Japan to open its ports to American trade

Saigo Takamori Leader of the Meiji Restoration who later opposed the new government's policies and led the Satsuma Rebellion

Tokugawa Iemitsu Third Tokugawa shogun, who created the system of restricting access to foreigners

Tokugawa Ieyasu Founder of the Tokugawa shogunate

Tokugawa Yoshinobu The last Tokugawa shogun, who failed to prevent the Meiji Restoration

Toyotomi Hideyoshi Warlord who unified Japan in the late 16th century

Timeline

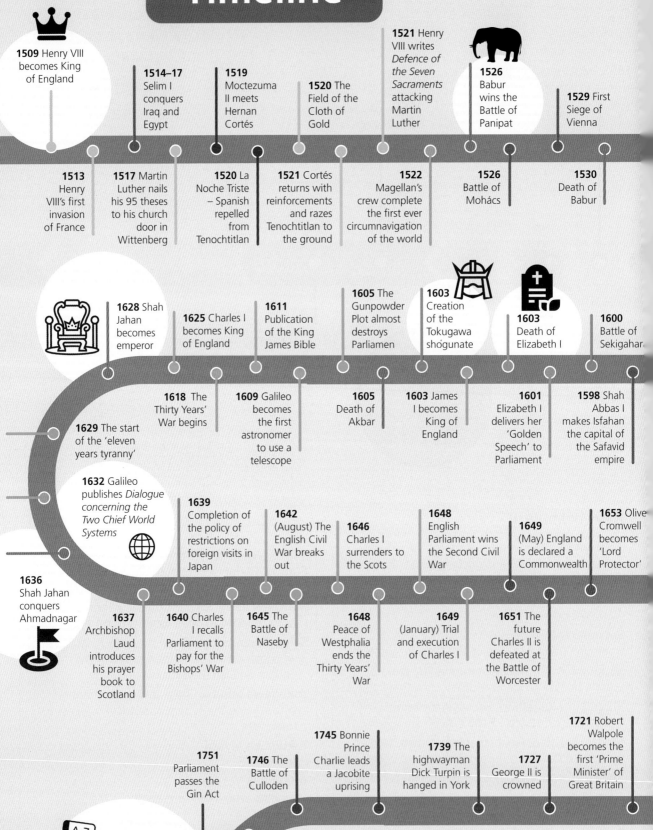

1509 Henry VIII becomes King of England

1514–17 Selim I conquers Iraq and Egypt

1519 Moctezuma II meets Hernan Cortés

1520 The Field of the Cloth of Gold

1521 Henry VIII writes *Defence of the Seven Sacraments* attacking Martin Luther

1526 Babur wins the Battle of Panipat

1529 First Siege of Vienna

1513 Henry VIII's first invasion of France

1517 Martin Luther nails his 95 theses to his church door in Wittenberg

1520 La Noche Triste – Spanish repelled from Tenochtitlan

1521 Cortés returns with reinforcements and razes Tenochtitlan to the ground

1522 Magellan's crew complete the first ever circumnavigation of the world

1526 Battle of Mohács

1530 Death of Babur

1628 Shah Jahan becomes emperor

1625 Charles I becomes King of England

1611 Publication of the King James Bible

1605 The Gunpowder Plot almost destroys Parliamen

1603 Creation of the Tokugawa shōgunate

1603 Death of Elizabeth I

1600 Battle of Sekigahar

1629 The start of the 'eleven years tyranny'

1618 The Thirty Years' War begins

1609 Galileo becomes the first astronomer to use a telescope

1605 Death of Akbar

1603 James I becomes King of England

1601 Elizabeth I delivers her 'Golden Speech' to Parliament

1598 Shah Abbas I makes Isfahan the capital of the Safavid empire

1632 Galileo publishes *Dialogue concerning the Two Chief World Systems*

1639 Completion of the policy of restrictions on foreign visits in Japan

1642 (August) The English Civil War breaks out

1646 Charles I surrenders to the Scots

1648 English Parliament wins the Second Civil War

1649 (May) England is declared a Commonwealth

1653 Olive Cromwell becomes 'Lord Protector'

1636 Shah Jahan conquers Ahmadnagar

1637 Archbishop Laud introduces his prayer book to Scotland

1640 Charles I recalls Parliament to pay for the Bishops' War

1645 The Battle of Naseby

1648 Peace of Westphalia ends the Thirty Years' War

1649 (January) Trial and execution of Charles I

1651 The future Charles II is defeated at the Battle of Worcester

1721 Robert Walpole becomes the first 'Prime Minister' of Great Britain

1745 Bonnie Prince Charlie leads a Jacobite uprising

1739 The highwayman Dick Turpin is hanged in York

1727 George II is crowned

1751 Parliament passes the Gin Act

1746 The Battle of Culloden

1755 Samuel Johnson publishes his dictionary of the English language

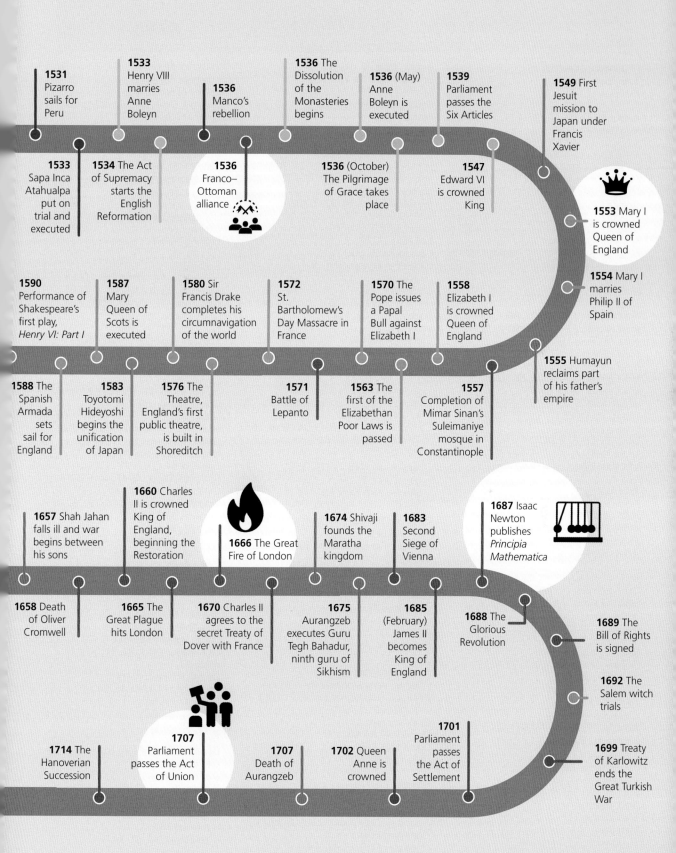

1531 Pizarro sails for Peru

1533 Henry VIII marries Anne Boleyn

1536 Manco's rebellion

1536 The Dissolution of the Monasteries begins

1536 (May) Anne Boleyn is executed

1539 Parliament passes the Six Articles

1549 First Jesuit mission to Japan under Francis Xavier

1533 Sapa Inca Atahualpa put on trial and executed

1534 The Act of Supremacy starts the English Reformation

1536 Franco–Ottoman alliance

1536 (October) The Pilgrimage of Grace takes place

1547 Edward VI is crowned King

1553 Mary I is crowned Queen of England

1554 Mary I marries Philip II of Spain

1590 Performance of Shakespeare's first play, *Henry VI: Part I*

1587 Mary Queen of Scots is executed

1580 Sir Francis Drake completes his circumnavigation of the world

1572 St. Bartholomew's Day Massacre in France

1570 The Pope issues a Papal Bull against Elizabeth I

1558 Elizabeth I is crowned Queen of England

1555 Humayun reclaims part of his father's empire

1588 The Spanish Armada sets sail for England

1583 Toyotomi Hideyoshi begins the unification of Japan

1576 The Theatre, England's first public theatre, is built in Shoreditch

1571 Battle of Lepanto

1563 The first of the Elizabethan Poor Laws is passed

1557 Completion of Mimar Sinan's Suleimaniye mosque in Constantinople

1657 Shah Jahan falls ill and war begins between his sons

1660 Charles II is crowned King of England, beginning the Restoration

1666 The Great Fire of London

1674 Shivaji founds the Maratha kingdom

1683 Second Siege of Vienna

1687 Isaac Newton publishes *Principia Mathematica*

1658 Death of Oliver Cromwell

1665 The Great Plague hits London

1670 Charles II agrees to the secret Treaty of Dover with France

1675 Aurangzeb executes Guru Tegh Bahadur, ninth guru of Sikhism

1685 (February) James II becomes King of England

1688 The Glorious Revolution

1689 The Bill of Rights is signed

1692 The Salem witch trials

1714 The Hanoverian Succession

1707 Parliament passes the Act of Union

1707 Death of Aurangzeb

1702 Queen Anne is crowned

1701 Parliament passes the Act of Settlement

1699 Treaty of Karlowitz ends the Great Turkish War

Index

Acknowledgments

Every effort has been made to trace copyright holders and to obtain their permission for the use of copyright material. The publishers will gladly receive any information enabling them to rectify any error or omission at the first opportunity. The publishers would like to thank the following for permission to reproduce copyright material:

(t = top, b = bottom, c = centre, l = left, r = right)

cover Deco / Alamy Stock Photo, p8 Heritage Image Partnership Ltd/Alamy, p9(b) Lebrecht Music and Arts Photo Library/Alamy, p9(t) GL Archive/Alamy, p11 imageBROKER/Alamy, p10(b) Ignatius Tan/Shutterstock, p10(t) FALKENSTEINFOTO/Alamy, p13 Ian Shaw/Alamy, p12(c) & 19(b) IanDagnall Computing/Alamy, p12(t) Mary Evans Picture Library/Alamy, p15 Badge of the Five Wounds of Christ (embroidered textile), English School, (16th century)/His Grace The Duke of Norfolk, Arundel Castle/Bridgeman Images, p12(b) GL Archive/Alamy, p14(b) Loop Images Ltd / Alamy Stock Photo, p14(t) Portrait of Sir Thomas More (1478-1535) (oil on panel), Holbein the Younger, Hans (1497/8-1543) (after)/National Portrait Gallery, London, UK/Bridgeman Images, p16(b) World History Archive/Alamy, p16(cb) World History Archive/Alamy, p16(ct) World History Archive/Alamy, p16(t) World History Archive/Alamy, p17(b) Photology1971/Shutterstock, p17(t) & 19(t) ACTIVE MUSEUM/Alamy, p20(b) Heritage Image Partnership Ltd/Alamy, p20(t) Ian Dagnall / Alamy Stock Photo, p21(b) Granger Historical Picture Archve/Alamy, p21(t) The burning of William Sawtre, illustration from 'Acts and Monuments' by John Foxe, ninth edition, pub. 1684 (litho), English School, (17th century)/Private Collection/The Stapleton Collection/Bridgeman Images, p22 Album / Alamy Stock Photo, p23(bc) World History Archive / Alamy Stock Photo, p23(br) Steve Sant / Alamy Stock Photo, p23(t) & 31 Ian Dagnall Commercial Collection / Alamy Stock Photo, p26 World History Archive / Alamy Stock Photo, p27 National Geographic Image Collection / Alamy Stock Photo, p24(b) World History Archive/Alamy, p24(t) Stocksnapper/Shutterstock, p25(b) Image Professionals GmbH / Alamy Stock Photo, p25(t) The Stapleton Collection / Bridgeman Images, p29, Fotosearch / Getty Images, p28(b) ACTIVE MUSEUM / ACTIVE ART / Alamy Stock Photo, p28(t) Bridgeman Images, p32 ACTIVE MUSEUM/Alamy, p33(t) Chronicle / Alamy Stock Photo, p35 Timewatch Images / Alamy Stock Photo, p34(b) Photo © Raffaello Bencini / Bridgeman Images, p34(t) & 43 Bridgeman Images, p36 © Ashmolean Museum / Bridgeman Images, p37 Bridgeman Images, p38 National Trust Photographic Library/Derrick E. Witty / Bridgeman Images, p39 © Look and Learn / Bridgeman Images, p33(b) © Look and Learn / Bridgeman Images, p40 Robert B. Miller/Shutterstock, p41(b) Bridgeman Images, p41(t) Bridgeman Images, p44 GL Archive / Alamy Stock Photo, p45(b) Stocktrek Images, Inc. / Alamy Stock Photo, p45(t) Heritage Image Partnership Ltd/Alamy, p47 Granger Historical Picture Archive / Alamy Stock Photo, p46(b) © Royal Collection / Royal Collection Trust © Her Majesty Queen Elizabeth II, 2021 / Bridgeman Images, p46(t) & 54 Niday Picture Library/Alamy, p48(b) & 55 19th era / Alamy Stock Photo, p48(t) World History Archive / Alamy Stock Photo, p49(b) GL Archive / Alamy Stock Photo, p49(t) Lebrecht Music & Arts / Alamy Stock Photo, p50 GL Archive / Alamy Stock Photo, p51(cr) GL Archive / Alamy Stock Photo, p51(t) TTstudio/Shutterstock, p53 © Royal Collection / Royal Collection Trust © Her Majesty Queen Elizabeth II, 2021 / Bridgeman Images, p52(c) Granger Historical Picture Archive / Alamy Stock Photo, p52(t) World History Archive / Alamy Stock Photo, p56 David Jackson / Alamy Stock Photo, p57 GL Archive / Alamy Stock Photo, p58(b) pcruciatti/Shutterstock.com, p58(t) Ian Dagnall / Alamy Stock Photo, p59 Everett - Art/Shutterstock, p60 GL Archive / Alamy Stock Photo, p61(br) StevanZZ/Shutterstock, p61(l) GL Archive / Alamy Stock Photo, p62(b) travellinglight / Alamy Stock Photo, p62(tr) The Artchives/Alamy, p63(b) & 67 Peter Horree / Alamy Stock Photo, p63(t) World History Archive / Alamy Stock Photo, p64 Lebrecht Music & Arts / Alamy Stock Photo, p65(b) Holmes Garden Photos / Alamy Stock Photo, p65(t) Heritage Image Partnership Ltd / Alamy Stock Photo, p69 Bridgeman Images, p68(b) Private Collection/© Look and Learn/Bridgeman Images, p68(t) Bridgeman Images, p70(b) or 71 (t) Everett Historical/Shutterstock, p70(c) & 78 (Spot image) imageBROKER/Alamy, p70(t) Nithid/Shutterstock, p71(b) Classic Image/Alamy, p73 Everett - Art/Shutterstock, p72(t) Dja65/Shutterstock, p74 Science History Images / Alamy Stock Photo, p75 The Print Collector / Alamy Stock Photo, p76 Helen Cowles / Alamy Stock Photo, p77 Science History Images / Alamy Stock Photo, p78 Classic Image/Alamy, p80 Shutterstock/Maximilian Wenzel, p81 Eman Kazemi / Alamy Stock Photo, p82 Science History Images / Alamy Stock Photo, p82 REUTERS / Alamy Stock Photo, p83 Niday Picture Library / Alamy Stock Photo, p84 Eteri Okrochelidze/Shutterstock, p85 Vanessa Volk/Shutterstock, p84 & 90 Jimlop collection / Alamy Stock Photo, p86 Everett Collection Inc / Alamy Stock Photo, p87 HeritagePics / Alamy Stock Photo, p88 The Granger Collection / Alamy Stock Photo, p89 Everett Collection, p92 Timewatch Images / Alamy Stock Photo, p92 Heracles Kritikos/Shutterstock, p93 Chris Hellier / Alamy Stock Photo, p94 IanDagnall Computing / Alamy Stock Photo, p95 Ruslan Kalnitsky/Shutterstock, p97 Hamdan Yoshida/Shutterstock, p97 Burak Budak/Shutterstock, p98 Granger Historical Picture Archive / Alamy Stock Photo, p99 The History Emporium / Alamy Stock Photo, p100 INTERFOTO / Alamy Stock Photo, p100 Sonia Halliday Photo Library / Alamy Stock Photo, p100 LizCoughlan / Shutterstock, p101 Volgi archive / Alamy Stock Photo, p101 Heritage Image Partnership Ltd / Alamy Stock Photo, p96 & 103 PRISMA ARCHIVO / Alamy Stock Photo, p104/105 World History Archive / Alamy Stock Photo, p107 World History Archive / Alamy Stock Photojavascript:onThumbClick('https://www.alamy.com/mediacomp/imagedetails.aspx?ref=F7ND42'), p108 Michele Burgess / Alamy Stock Photo, p109 V&A Images / Alamy Stock Photo, p110 Historic Images / Alamy Stock Photo, p111 imageBROKER / Alamy Stock Photo, p111 Shutterstock/YURY TARANIK, p112 IndiaPicture / Alamy Stock Photo, p113 ephotocorp / Alamy Stock Photo, p106 & 114 Granger Historical Picture Archive / Alamy Stock Photo, p117 Jon Bower- art and museums / Alamy Stock Photo, p118 CPA Media Pte Ltd / Alamy Stock Photo, p119 Shutterstock/Dilhani Manuweera, p120 Universal Images Group North America LLC / Alamy Stock Photo, p121 Shutterstock/Luciano Mortula - LGM, p122 Old Paper Studios / Alamy Stock Photo, p123 Historic Collection / Alamy Stock Photo, p124 Pictorial Press Ltd / Alamy Stock Photo, p125 Granger Historical Picture Archive / Alamy Stock Photo, p116 & 127 GL Archive / Alamy Stock Photo,